MEMORIES AND PORTRAITS

MEMORIES AND PORTRAITS

ROBERT LOUIS STEVENSON

RICHARD DREW PUBLISHING
GLASGOW

First published 1887

This edition first published 1990 by
Richard Drew Publishing Ltd
6 Clairmont Gardens
Glasgow G3 7LW Scotland

The publisher wishes to acknowledge the financial assistance of the Scottish Arts Council in the publication of this work.

British Library Cataloguing in Publication Data
Stevenson, Robert Louis, *1850-1894*
Memories and portraits. – (The Scottish Collection.)
1. English literature. Stevenson, Robert Louis, 1850-1894
I. Title II. Series
828′.809

ISBN 0-86267-273-2

Printed and bound in Great Britain by
Cox & Wyman Ltd, Reading

To My Mother
in the name of past joy and present sorrow
I dedicate
these memories and portraits

SS 'Ludgate Hill'
within sight of Cape Race

NOTE

This volume of papers, unconnected as they are, it will be better to read through from the beginning, rather than dip into at random. A certain thread of meaning binds them. Memories of childhood and youth, portraits of those who have gone before us in the battle — taken together, they build up a face that 'I have loved long since and lost awhile,' the face of what was once myself. This has come by accident; I had no design at first to be autobiographical; I was but led away by the charm of beloved memories and by regret for the irrevocable dead; and when my own young face (which is a face of the dead also) began to appear in the well as by a kind of magic, I was the first to be surprised at the occurrence.

My grandfather the pious child, my father the idle eager sentimental youth, I have thus unconsciously exposed. Of their descendant, the person of to-day, I wish to keep the secret: not because I love him better, but because, with him, I am still in a business partnership, and cannot divide interests.

Of the papers which make up the volume, some have appeared already in *The Cornhill*, *Longmans*, *Scribner's*, *The English Illustrated*, *The Magazine of Art*, *The Contemporary Review*; three are here in print for the first time; and two others have enjoyed only what may be regarded as a private circulation.

R. L. S.

INTRODUCTION

MEMORIES AND PORTRAITS can be read as Robert Louis Stevenson's own introduction to his work up to 1887. It was published in the autumn of that year, not long after Stevenson himself had left Scotland, a departure that brought to a close the crucially formative experience of coming of age in the northern part of Victorian Britain. The nature of this experience is examined and reflected in the essays collected in this volume, most of which had been published in periodicals during the previous five years.

By the time *Memories and Portraits* was published Stevenson had established his reputation as a writer. Between them *Treasure Island, Strange Case of Dr. Jekyll and Mr Hyde* and *Kidnapped* had brought him respect and popularity; he was known and enjoyed also as a writer of short stories, essays and travel books. And he was very highly regarded by a number of his contemporaries, including Henry James and Leslie Stephen, editor of the *Cornhill Magazine* which published three of the essays here. He was thought of by them as a writer moving towards the accomplishment of great things, and he was very aware that much was expected of him.

The year 1887 was a turning point. The death of his father lightened the burden of parental and Calvinist authority, and although he never shed the influence of either he gained a measure of psychological freedom. *Memories and Portraits* was a conscious tribute to the life that had gone before. The book is dedicated to his mother, but thoughts of his father were certainly in his mind as he put the collection together. In the essay on his father, Thomas Stevenson, civil engineer, he records the personality and achievements of a difficult and contradictory man, of 'blended sternness and softness', melancholy, passionate, wise and prejudiced. 'He never accepted the conditions of man's life or his own character', Stevenson said of him, and towards the end of his own life RLS was saying something very similar about himself. Like his father he, too, wrestled continually with the confusions of human emotion and the morality of action. Like his father, he sometimes felt he had lost his way in the labyrinths of life.

The essay on Thomas Stevenson comes, appropriately, half way through the book. Before and after come pieces that are mainly lighter in tone, though there are often dark eddies beneath the surface. They celebrate rather different aspects of Stevenson's shaping experiences. It is this weaving together of contrasting strands that makes *Memories and Portraits* such a rewarding collection. He points us to episodes, people and places that influenced him: his grandfather's manse at Colinton, his delight in Skelt's model theatre, a Pentland shepherd and his dogs, good companionship and good conversation. We catch glimpses of his family, his childhood, his friends. And throughout there are the powerful undercurrents: his profound involvement with Scotland, past and present, his rich response to experience, and the instinctive perception of reality as the basis of romance.

These are the ingredients of his inspiration as a writer. He drew on his own childhood and the unhampered latitude of the child's imagination. His fascination with his own origins and family history went hand in hand with an almost obsessive interest in the pivotal conflicts and divisions of Scottish history. Many of the essays here reflect his particular responsiveness to place, which is so powerful a feature of his fiction. In 'A Gossip on Romance' he talks of 'the genius of place': 'certain dank gardens cry aloud for a murder; certain old houses demand to be haunted; certain coasts are set apart for a shipwreck'. We can instantly recognise the seeds of his own fiction, and when he goes on to discuss the suggestiveness of the Hawes Inn in Queensferry, and the need of a story 'to express the meaning of that inn', we can appreciate the genesis of *Kidnapped*, in which the Hawes plays a vital role.

Running through most of these pieces is Stevenson's absorption of Scotland's history. For him the past continually features in the present, his own life was inseparable from that of his ancestors. Wherever he was he saw not only the observable present but the enactment of ancient dramas. In 'The Foreigner at Home', where he has much to say about the Scottish character, he writes of the way Scotland's history grows in the child's mind from story and from observation.

> A Scottish child hears much of shipwreck, outlying iron skerries, pitiless breakers, and the great sea-lights; much of heathery mountains, wild clans, and hunted Covenanters. Breaths come to him in song of the distant Cheviots and the ring of foraying hoofs. He glories in the hard-fisted forefathers, of the iron girdle and handful of oatmeal, who rode so swiftly and lived so sparely on their raids. Poverty, ill-

luck, enterprise, and constant resolution are the fibres of the legend of his country's history.

He is, of course, writing here about himself, highlighting his own response to the past as well as the features that contribute to Scotland's particular identity.

All of these elements nourished Stevenson's imagination, and the essays in *Memories and Portraits* help us to understand the process of both generation and creation which directed his writing. He began with reality, but he saw always the possibilities of romance. It was not that he abandoned the real for the romantic, but that he had a striking ability to draw out of the real what was most suggestive of challenge and action. In the two final essays he provides an insight into his understanding of romance, an understanding that grows out of his awareness of his own needs as a reader. In 'A Gossip on Romance' he writes 'the great creative writer shows us the realisation and the apotheosis of the day-dreams of common men. His stories may be nourished with the realities of life, but their true mark is to satisfy the nameless longings of the reader, and to obey the ideal laws of the day-dream.' This acknowledgement of the importance of the 'day-dream', of freedom of the imagination, of story-telling for the sheer pleasure of blending character and incident, cheerfully undermines more solemn approaches to literature, and at the same time emphasises its radical function.

Stevenson's views on fiction both echoed those of some of his contemporaries and brought him into a debate about the nature and potential of fiction. There were those who felt that fiction needed revitalising, that it was time to move away from a preoccupation with a polite domestic scene—what Stevenson describes as 'the clink of teaspoons and the accents of the curate'. 'It is thought clever,' he goes on, 'to write a novel with no story at all, or at least with a very dull one.' Stevenson's reaction against this was part of what encouraged Leslie Stephen to see him as the talent that would rescue British fiction from prosaic manoeuvres against a dreary background.

The 1880s debate about fiction is of great significance not only to the student of literature, but to anyone with an interest in the period and its cultural developments. At its heart was a concern with realism, with whether art, of any kind, could or should attempt to represent reality. The nineteenth century had seen the rise of the naturalistic painting as well as the naturalistic novel. It had seen the birth and growth of photography, and the advance of journalism and documentary writing. The expansion of publishing, the proliferation of magazines and journals (which provided more outlets for writers like Stevenson) brought words and pictures to a wider audience. Revolutionary developments in communications, the appearance of the telegraph, the typewriter, the telephone, helped to make information more accessible. This was the context of sometimes heated discussions about the relationship between life and art, between perception and expression.

Stevenson's contribution was to argue that it was not possible for art to represent reality, that life was just too intricate and hazardous. He took issue with Henry James, who later became a close friend: James believed that the novel should 'compete with life', should attempt to express and explore life in all its complexity. Stevenson replied:

> Life goes before us, infinite in complication; attended by the most various and surprising meteors; appealing at once to the eye, to the ear, to the mind . . . It combines and employs in its manifestation the method and material, not of one art only, but of all the arts . . . literature does but drily indicate that wealth of incident, of moral obligation, of virtue, vice, action, rapture and agony, with which it teems.

Art is inevitably selective, Stevenson felt. Life, 'monstrous, infinite, illogical, abrupt and poignant' provided the raw material for an art that, by its nature, was 'neat, finite, self-contained, rational, flowing and emasculate'. The compensation for this drastic limitation is passion; that, Stevenson considered, was the key to the novelist's achievement.

Over the next few years Stevenson would modify his views, partly as a result of distancing himself from Scotland and through exposure to a different kind of reality, but he may also have been influenced by his experience of the new technology. He made use of the telegraph, benefited directly from improved communications, and became a keen photographer. All this was part of what made 1887 a turning point.

He began to feel that the writer had a responsibility to convey what he saw and understood, rather than to distil from it the essence of a good story. In fact, he found that he could do both—his story 'The Beach of Falesá' is a good example of his success. Stevenson often suggested that it was the writer's task to entertain, and such comments have tempted readers to assume that his attitude to his craft was not entirely serious. The opposite was the case. He cared profoundly about his work, but cared as a *reader* as well as a writer. As a reader he expected literature to transport the imagination; as a writer he was guided by a profoundly moral sensibility, and wanted to teach, or preach, and enlighten. At his best he does both.

Memories and Portraits documents aspects of Stevenson's experience of life and literature, and is full of illumination of his other work. The essays have a special interest in this wider context, but they can also be read and enjoyed for their own sake. They are the product of a meticulous craftsman, who handled words with scrupulous care, but at the same time wanted to impress and to avoid tired images and ideas. Sometimes in his effort to paint a scene freshly or present a thought in a new light he tries too hard, but by the 1880s he had matured beyond the more brittle artifice of his early work. He often introduces the first person, and he has been criticised for creating a determinedly positive and optimistic persona, a kind of disguise which shields the true author. But, as he himself pointed out, writing is a process of selection, and like all writers he presented a chosen face to the world. *Memories and Portraits* is not the complete Stevenson, but it is part of the real Stevenson.

As a writer, of fiction, non-fiction and poetry, Stevenson drew on anything and everything that came to hand. The whole of human experience, past and present, fascinated him, and although the twin pressures of Calvinist and Victorian expectations sometimes silenced him, he challenged many of the assumptions of his times. The carefulness of his writing does not mask the flexibility, indeed at times the anarchy, of his mind, or the vivid free association that we find in essays such as 'Old Mortality' or 'Pastoral'. These are amongst the qualities that give Stevenson a distinctive voice and that make him so enjoyable to read more than a century on.

Stevenson suggests, in his 'Note' to the volume, that the essays should be read in order, for, he says, 'a certain thread of meaning binds them'. They do provide a kind of chronicle and, although there are other essays in other volumes that offer glimpses of the growing consciousness and the developing writer, *Memories and Portraits* is the only collection that provides, not exactly a narrative, but a coherent tapestry of shaping experiences. Some of the essays have since appeared in different contexts but, however rewarding, transplantation loses the sense of connection and continuity.

Reading the essays today the underlying theme that emerges most strongly is that of mortality on the one hand and the compensatory power of literature on the other. Whatever the subject, Stevenson is writing either of people and human activity and the inevitable movement from now to then, or of the way words can capture, preserve and recreate. *Memories and Portraits* is not fiction, but it is story telling, and story telling is the giving of life, in Stevenson's eyes a creativity that was a powerful counterweight to impermanence.

Jenni Calder

CONTENTS

MEMORIES AND PORTRAITS

I

THE FOREIGNER AT HOME

"This is no' my ain house;
I ken by the biggin' o't."

TWO recent books,* one by Mr. Grant White on England, one on France by the diabolically clever Mr. Hillebrand, may well have set people thinking on the divisions of races and nations. Such thoughts should arise with particular congruity and force to inhabitants of that United Kingdom, peopled from so many different stocks, babbling so many different dialects, and offering in its extent such singular contrasts, from the busiest over-population to the unkindliest desert, from the Black Country to the Moor of Rannoch. It is not only when we cross the seas that we go abroad; there are foreign parts of England; and the race that has conquered so wide an empire has not yet managed to assimilate the islands whence she sprang. Ireland, Wales, and the Scottish mountains still cling, in part, to their

* 1881.

old Gaelic speech. It was but the other day that English triumphed in Cornwall, and they still show in Mousehole, on St. Michael's Bay, the house of the last Cornish-speaking woman. English itself, which will now frank the traveller through the most of North America, through the greater South Sea Islands, in India, along much of the coast of Africa, and in the ports of China and Japan, is still to be heard, in its home country, in half a hundred varying stages of transition. You may go all over the States, and —setting aside the actual intrusion and influence of foreigners, negro, French, or Chinese—you shall scarce meet with so marked a difference of accent as in the forty miles between Edinburgh and Glasgow, or of dialect as in the hundred miles between Edinburgh and Aberdeen. Book English has gone round the world, but at home we still preserve the racy idioms of our fathers, and every county, in some parts every dale, has its own quality of speech, vocal or verbal. In like manner, local custom and prejudice, even local religion and local law, linger on into the latter end of the nineteenth century—*imperia in imperio*, foreign things at home.

In spite of these promptings to reflection, ignorance of his neighbours is the character of the typical John Bull. His is a domineering nature, steady in fight, imperious to command, but neither curious nor quick about the life of others. In French colonies, and still more in the Dutch, I have read that there is an immediate and lively contact between the dominant and the dominated race, that a certain sympathy is begotten, or at least a transfusion of prejudices, making life easier for both. But the Englishman sits apart, bursting with pride and ignorance. He figures among his vassals in the hour of peace with the same disdainful air that led him on to victory. A passing enthusiasm for some foreign art or fashion may deceive the world, it cannot impose upon his intimates. He may be amused by a foreigner as by a monkey, but he will never condescend to study him with any patience. Miss Bird, an authoress with whom I profess myself in love, declares all the viands of Japan to be uneatable—a staggering pretension. So, when the Prince of Wales's marriage was celebrated at Mentone by a dinner to the Mentonese, it was proposed to give them solid English fare—roast beef and plum pudding, and no tomfoolery. Here we have either pole of the Britannic folly. We will not eat the food of any foreigner; nor, when we have the chance, will we suffer him to eat of it himself. The same spirit inspired Miss Bird's American missionaries, who had come thousands of miles to change the faith of Japan, and openly professed their ignorance of the religions they were trying to supplant.

I quote an American in this connection without scruple. Uncle Sam is better than John Bull, but he is tarred with the English stick. For Mr. Grant White the States are the New England States and nothing more. He wonders at the amount of drinking in London; let him try San Francisco. He wittily reproves English ignorance as to the status of women in America; but has he not himself forgotten Wyoming? The name Yankee, of which he is so tenacious, is used over the most of the great Union as a term of reproach. The Yankee States, of which he is so staunch a subject, are but a drop in the bucket. And we find in his book a vast virgin ignorance of the life and prospects of America; every view partial, parochial, not raised to the horizon; the moral feeling proper, at the largest, to a clique of States; and the whole scope and atmosphere not American but merely Yankee. I will go far beyond him in reprobating the assumption and the incivility of my country-folk to their cousins from beyond the sea; I grill in my blood over the silly rudeness of our newspaper articles; and I do not know where to look when I find myself in company with an American and see my countrymen unbending to him as to a performing dog. But in the case of Mr. Grant White example were better than precept. Wyoming is, after all, more readily accessible to Mr. White than Boston to the English, and the New England self-sufficiency no better justified than the Britannic.

It is so, perhaps, in all countries; perhaps in all, men are most ignorant of the foreigners at home. John Bull is ignorant of the States; he is probably ignorant of India; but considering his opportunities, he is far more ignorant of countries nearer his own door. There is one country, for instance—its frontier not so far from London, its people closely akin, its language the same in all essentials with the English—of which I will go bail he knows nothing. His ignorance of the sister kingdom cannot be described; it can only be illustrated by anecdote. I once travelled with a man of plausible manners and good intelligence—a University man, as the phrase goes—a man, besides, who had taken his degree in life and knew a thing or two about the age we live in. We were deep in talk, whirling between Peterborough and London; among other things, he began to describe some piece of legal injustice he had recently encountered, and I observed in my innocence that things were not so in Scotland. "I beg your pardon," said he, "this is a matter of law." He had never heard of the Scots law; nor did he choose to be informed. The law was the same for the whole country, he told me roundly; every child knew that. At last, to settle matters, I explained to him that I was a member of a Scottish legal body, and had stood the brunt of an examination in the very law in question. Thereupon he looked me for a moment full in the face and dropped the conversation. This is a monstrous instance, if you like, but it does not stand alone in the experience of Scots.

England and Scotland differ, indeed, in law, in history, in religion, in education, and in the very look of nature and men's faces, not always widely, but always trenchantly. Many particulars that struck Mr. Grant White, a Yankee, struck me, a Scot, no less forcibly; he and I felt ourselves foreigners on many common provocations. A Scotchman may tramp the better part of Europe and the United States, and never again receive so vivid an impression of foreign travel and strange lands and manners as on his first excursion into England. The change from a hilly to a level country strikes him with delighted wonder. Along the flat horizon there arise the frequent venerable towers of churches. He sees at the end of airy vistas the revolution of the windmill sails. He may go where he pleases in the future; he may see Alps, and Pyramids, and lions; but it will be hard to beat the pleasure of that moment. There are, indeed, few merrier spectacles than that of many windmills bickering together in a fresh breeze over a woody country; their halting alacrity of movement, their pleasant business, making bread all day with uncouth gesticulations, their air, gigantically human, as of a creature half alive, put a spirit of romance into the tamest landscape. When the Scotch child sees them first he falls immediately in love; and from that time forward windmills keep turning in his dreams. And so, in their degree, with every feature of the life and landscape. The warm, habitable age of towns and hamlets, the green, settled, ancient look of the country; the lush hedgerows, stiles, and privy pathways in the fields; the sluggish, brimming rivers; chalk and smock-frocks; chimes of bells and the rapid, pertly-sounding English speech—they are all new to the curiosity;

they are all set to English airs in the child's story that he tells himself at night. The sharp edge of novelty wears off; the feeling is scotched, but I doubt whether it is ever killed. Rather it keeps returning, ever the more rarely and strangely, and even in scenes to which you have been long accustomed suddenly awakes and gives a relish to enjoyment or heightens the sense of isolation.

One thing especially continues unfamiliar to the Scotchman's eye—the domestic architecture, the look of streets and buildings; the quaint, venerable age of many, and the thin walls and warm colouring of all. We have, in Scotland, far fewer ancient buildings, above all in country places; and those that we have are all of hewn or harled masonry. Wood has been sparingly used in their construction; the window-frames are sunken in the wall, not flat to the front, as in England; the roofs are steeper-pitched; even a hill farm will have a massy, square, cold and permanent appearance. English houses, in comparison, have the look of cardboard toys, such as a puff might shatter. And to this the Scotchman never becomes used. His eye can never rest consciously on one of these brick houses—rickles of brick, as he might call them—or on one of these flat-chested streets, but he is instantly reminded where he is, and instantly travels back in fancy to his home. "This is no' my ain house; I ken by the biggin' o't." And yet perhaps it is his own, bought with his own money, the key of it long polished in his pocket; but it has not yet, and never will be, thoroughly adopted by his imagination; nor does he cease to remember that, in the whole length and breadth of his native country, there was no building even distantly resembling it.

But it is not alone in scenery and architecture that we count England foreign. The constitution of society, the very pillars of the empire, surprise and even pain us. The dull, neglected peasant, sunk in matter, insolent, gross and servile, makes a startling contrast with our own long-legged, long-headed, thoughtful, Bible-quoting ploughman. A week or two in such a place as Suffolk leaves the Scotchman gasping. It seems incredible that within the boundaries of his own island a class should have been thus forgotten. Even the educated and intelligent, who hold our own opinions and speak in our own words, yet seem to hold them with a difference or from another reason, and to speak on all things with less interest and conviction. The first shock of English society is like a cold plunge. It is possible that the Scot comes looking for too much, and to be sure his first experiment will be in the wrong direction. Yet surely his complaint is grounded; surely the speech of Englishmen is too often lacking in generous ardour, the better part of the man too often withheld from the social commerce, and the contact of mind with mind evaded as with terror. A Scotch peasant will talk more liberally out of his own experience. He will not put you by with conversational counters and small jests; he will give you the best of himself, like one interested in life and man's chief end. A Scotchman is vain, interested in himself and others, eager for sympathy, setting forth his thoughts and experience in the best light. The egoism of the Englishman is self-contained. He does not seek to proselytise. He takes no interest in Scotland or the Scotch, and, what is the unkindest cut of all, he does not care to justify his indifference. Give him the wages of going on and being an Englishman, that is all he asks; and in the meantime, while you continue to associate, he would rather not be reminded of your baser origin. Compared with the grand, tree-like self-sufficiency of his demeanour, the vanity and curiosity of the Scot seem uneasy, vulgar, and immodest. That you should continually try to establish human and serious relations, that you should actually feel an interest in John Bull, and desire and invite a return of interest from him, may argue something more awake and lively in your mind, but it still puts you in the attitude of a suitor and a poor relation. Thus even the lowest class of the educated English towers over a Scotchman by the head and shoulders.

Different indeed is the atmosphere in which Scotch and English youth begin to look about them, come to themselves in life, and gather up those first apprehensions which are the material of future thought and, to a great extent, the rule of future conduct. I have been to school in both countries, and I found, in the boys of the North, something at once rougher and more tender, at once more reserve and more expansion, a greater habitual distance chequered by glimpses of a nearer intimacy, and on the whole wider extremes of temperament and sensibility. The boy of the South seems more wholesome, but less thoughtful; he gives himself to games as to a business, striving to excel, but is not readily transported by imagination; the type remains with me as cleaner in mind and body, more active, fonder of eating, endowed with a lesser and a less romantic sense of life and of the future, and more immersed in present circumstances. And certainly, for one thing, English boys are younger for their age. Sabbath observance makes a series of grim, and perhaps serviceable, pauses in the tenor of Scotch boyhood—days of great stillness and solitude for the rebellious mind, when in the dearth of books and play, and in the intervals of studying the Shorter Catechism, the intellect and senses prey upon and test each other. The typical English Sunday, with the huge midday dinner and the plethoric afternoon, leads perhaps to different results. About the very cradle of the Scot there goes a hum of metaphysical divinity; and the whole of two divergent systems is summed up, not merely speciously, in the two first questions of the rival catechisms, the English tritely inquiring, "What is your name?" the Scottish striking at the very roots of life with, "What is the chief end of man ?" and answering nobly, if obscurely, "To glorify God and to enjoy Him for ever." I do not wish to make an idol of the Shorter Catechism; but the fact of such a question being asked opens to us Scotch a great field of speculation; and the fact that it is asked of all of us, from the peer to the ploughboy, binds us more nearly together. No Englishman of Byron's age, character and history, would have had patience for long theological discussions on the way to fight for Greece; but the daft Gordon blood and the Aberdonian schooldays kept their influence to the end. We have spoken of the material conditions; nor need much more be said of these: of the land lying everywhere more exposed, of the wind always louder and bleaker, of the black, roaring winters, of the gloom of high-lying, old stone cities, imminent on the windy seaboard; compared with the level streets, the warm colouring of the brick, the domestic quaintness of the architecture, among which English children begin to grow up and come to themselves in life. As the stage of the University approaches, the contrast becomes more express. The English lad goes to Oxford or Cambridge; there, in an ideal world of gardens, to lead a semi-scenic life, costumed, disciplined and drilled by proctors. Nor is this to be regarded merely as a stage of education; it is a piece of privilege besides, and a step that separates him further from the bulk of his compatriots. At an earlier age the Scottish lad begins his greatly different experience of crowded class-rooms, of a gaunt quadrangle, of a bell hourly booming over the traffic of the city to recall him from the public-house where he has been lunching, or the streets where he has been wandering fancy-free. His college life has little of restraint, and nothing of necessary gentility. He will find no quiet clique of the exclusive, studious and cultured; no rotten borough of the arts. All classes rub shoulders on the greasy benches. The raffish young gentleman in gloves must measure his scholarship with the plain, clownish laddie from the parish school. They separate, at the session's end, one to smoke cigars about a watering-place, the other to resume the labours of the field beside his peasant family. The first muster of a college class in Scotland is a scene of curious and painful interest; so many lads, fresh from the heather, hang round the stove in cloddish embarrassment, ruffled by the presence of their smarter comrades, and afraid of the sound of their own rustic voices. It was in these early days, I think, that Professor Blackie won the affection of his pupils, putting these uncouth, umbrageous students at their ease with ready human geniality. Thus, at least, we have a healthy democratic atmosphere to breathe in while at work; even when there is no cordiality there is always a juxtaposition of the different classes, and in the competition of study the intellectual power of each is plainly demonstrated to the other. Our tasks ended, we of the North go forth as freemen into the humming, lamplit city. At five o'clock you may see the last of us hiving from the college gates, in the glare of the shop windows, under the green glimmer of the winter sunset. The frost tingles in our blood; no proctor lies in wait to intercept us; till the bell sounds again, we are the masters of the world; and some portion of our lives is always Saturday, *la trêve de Dieu.*

Nor must we omit the sense of the nature of his country and his country's history gradually growing in the child's mind from story and from observation. A Scottish child hears much of shipwreck, outlying iron skerries, pitiless breakers, and great sea-lights; much of heathery mountains, wild clans, and hunted Covenanters. Breaths come to him in song of the distant Cheviots and the ring of foraying hoofs. He glories in his hard-fisted forefathers, of the iron girdle and the handful of oatmeal, who rode so swiftly and lived so sparely on their raids. Poverty, ill-luck, enterprise, and constant resolution are the fibres of the legend of his country's history. The heroes and kings of Scotland have been tragically fated; the most marking incidents in Scottish history—Flodden, Darien, or the Forty-five—were still either failures or defeats; and the fall of Wallace and the repeated reverses of the Bruce combine with the very smallness of the country to teach rather a moral than a material criterion for life. Britain is altogether small, the mere taproot of her extended empire: Scotland, again, which alone the Scottish boy adopts in his imagination, is but a little part of that, and avowedly cold, sterile and unpopulous. It is not so for nothing. I once seemed to have perceived in an American boy a greater readiness of sympathy for lands that are great, and rich, and growing, like his own. It proved to be quite otherwise: a mere dumb piece of boyish romance, that I had lacked penetration to divine. But the error serves the purpose of my argument; for I am sure, at least, that the heart of young Scotland will be always touched more nearly by paucity of number and Spartan poverty of life.

So we may argue, and yet the difference is not explained. That Shorter Catechism which I took as being so typical of Scotland, was yet composed in the city of Westminster. The division of races is more sharply marked within the borders of Scotland itself than between the countries. Galloway and Buchan, Lothian and Lochaber, are like foreign parts; yet you may choose a man from any of them, and, ten to one, he shall prove to have the headmark of a Scot. A century and a half ago the Highlander wore a different costume, spoke a different language, worshipped in another church, held different morals, and obeyed a different social constitution from his fellow-countrymen either of the south or north. Even the English, it is recorded, did not loathe the Highlander and the Highland costume as they were loathed by the remainder of the Scotch. Yet the Highlander felt himself a Scot. He would willingly raid into the Scotch lowlands; but his courage failed him at the border, and he regarded England as a perilous, unhomely land. When the Black Watch, after years of foreign service, returned to Scotland, veterans leaped out and kissed the earth at Port Patrick. They had been in Ireland, stationed among men of their own race and language, where they were well liked and treated with affection; but it was the soil of Galloway that they kissed at the extreme end of the hostile lowlands, among a people who did not understand their speech, and who had hated, harried, and hanged them since the dawn of history. Last, and perhaps most curious, the sons of chieftains were often educated on the continent of Europe. They went abroad speaking Gaelic; they returned speaking, not English, but the broad dialect of Scotland. Now, what idea had they in their minds when they thus, in thought, identified themselves with their ancestral enemies? What was the sense in which they were Scotch and not English, or Scotch and not Irish? Can a bare name be thus influential on the minds and affections of men, and a political aggregation blind them to the nature of facts? The story of the Austrian Empire would seem to answer, No; the far more galling business of Ireland clenches the negative from nearer home. Is it common education, common morals, a common language or a common faith, that join men into nations? There were practically none of these in the case we are considering.

The fact remains: in spite of the difference of blood and language, the Lowlander feels himself the sentimental countryman of the Highlander. When they meet abroad, they fall upon each other's necks in spirit; even at home there is a kind of clannish intimacy in their talk. But from his compatriot in the south the Lowlander stands consciously apart. He has had a different training; he obeys different laws; he makes his will in other terms, is otherwise divorced and married; his eyes are not at home in an English landscape or with English houses; his ear continues to remark the English speech; and even though his tongue acquire the Southern knack, he will still have a strong Scotch accent of the mind.

II

Some College Memories *

I AM asked to write something (it is not specifically stated what) to the profit and glory of my *Alma Mater ;* and the fact is I seem to be in very nearly the same case with those who addressed me, for while I am willing enough to write something, I know not what to write. Only one point I see, that if I am to write at all, it should be of the University itself and my own days under its shadow ; of the things that are still the same and of those that are already changed : such talk, in short, as would pass naturally between a student of to-day and one of yesterday, supposing them to meet and grow confidential.

The generations pass away swiftly enough on the high seas of life ; more swiftly still in the little bubbling backwater of the quadrangle ; so that we see there, on a scale startlinglydiminished, the flight of time and the succession of men. I looked for my name the other day in last year's case-book of the Speculative. Naturally enough I looked for it near the end ; it was not there,

* Written for the "Book" of the Edinburgh University Union Fancy Fair.

nor yet in the next column, so that I began to think it had been dropped at press; and when at last I found it, mounted on the shoulders of so many successors, and looking in that posture like the name of a man of ninety, I was conscious of some of the dignity of years. This kind of dignity of temporal precession is likely, with prolonged life, to become more familiar, possibly less welcome; but I felt it strongly then, it is strongly on me now, and I am the more emboldened to speak with my successors in the tone of a parent and a praiser of things past.

For, indeed, that which they attend is but a fallen University; it has doubtless some remains of good, for human institutions decline by gradual stages; but decline, in spite of all seeming embellishments, it does; and what is perhaps more singular, began to do so when I ceased to be a student. Thus, by an odd chance, I had the very last of the very best of *Alma Mater;* the same thing, I hear (which makes it the more strange), had previously happened to my father; and if they are good and do not die, something not at all unsimilar will be found in time to have befallen my successors of to-day. Of the specific points of change, of advantage in the past, of shortcoming in the present, I must own that, on a near examination, they look wondrous cloudy. The chief and far the most lamentable change is the absence of a certain lean, ugly, idle, unpopular student, whose presence was for me the gist and heart of the whole matter; whose changing humours, fine occasional purposes of good, flinching acceptance of evil, shiverings on wet, east-windy, morning journeys up to class, infinite yawnings during lecture and unquenchable gusto in the delights of truantry, made up the sunshine and shadow of my college life. You cannot fancy what you missed in missing him; his virtues, I make sure, are inconceivable to his successors, just as they were apparently concealed from his contemporaries, for I was practically alone in the pleasure I had in his society. Poor soul, I remember how much he was cast down at times, and how life (which had not yet begun) seemed to be already at an end, and hope quite dead, and misfortune and dishonour, like physical presences, dogging him as he went. And it may be worth while to add that these clouds rolled away in their season, and that all clouds roll away at last, and the troubles of youth in particular are things but of a moment. So this student, whom I have in my eye, took his full share of these concerns, and that very largely by his own fault; but he still clung to his fortune, and in the midst of much misconduct, kept on in his own way learning how to work; and at last, to his wonder, escaped out of the stage of studentship not openly shamed; leaving behind him the University of Edinburgh shorn of a good deal of its interest for myself.

But while he is (in more senses than one) the first person, he is by no means the only one whom I regret, or whom the students of to-day, if they knew what they had lost would regret also. They have still Tait, to be sure—long may they have him!—and they have still Tait's class-room cupola and all; but think of what a different place it was when this youth of mine (at least on roll days) would be present on the benches, and, at the near end of the platform, Lindsay senior * was airing his robust old age. It is possible my successors may have never even heard of Old Lindsay; but when he went, a link snapped with the last century. He had something of a rustic air, sturdy and fresh and plain; he spoke with a ripe east-country accent, which I used to admire; his reminiscences were all of journeys on foot or highways busy with post-chaises—a Scotland before steam; he had seen the coal fire on the Isle of May, and he regaled me with tales of my own grandfather. Thus he was for me a mirror of things perished; it was only in his memory that I could see the huge shock of flames of the May beacon stream to leeward, and the watchers, as they fed the fire, lay hold unscorched of the windward bars of the furnace; it was only thus that I could see my grandfather driving swiftly in a gig along the seaboard road from Pittenweem to Crail, and for all his business hurry, drawing up to speak good-humouredly with those he met. And now, in his turn, Lindsay is gone also; inhabits only the memories of other men, till these shall follow

* Professor Tait's laboratory assistant.

him; and figures in my reminiscences as my grandfather figured in his.

To-day, again, they have Professor Butcher, and I hear he has a prodigious deal of Greek; and they have Professor Chrystal, who is a man filled with the mathematics. And doubtless these are set-offs. But they cannot change the fact that Professor Blackie has retired, and that Professor Kelland is dead. No man's education is complete or truly liberal who knew not Kelland. There were unutterable lessons in the mere sight of that frail old clerical gentleman, lively as a boy, kind like a fairy godfather, and keeping perfect order in his class by the spell of that very kindness. I have heard him drift into reminiscences in class time, though not for long, and give us glimpses of old-world life in out-of-the-way English parishes when he was young; thus playing the same part as Lindsay—the part of the surviving memory, signalling out of the dark backward and abysm of time the images of perished things. But it was a part that scarce became him; he somehow lacked the means; for all his silver hair and worn face, he was not truly old; and he had too much of the unrest and petulant fire of youth, and too much invincible innocence of mind, to play the veteran well. The time to measure him best, to taste (in the old phrase) his gracious nature, was when he received his class at home. What a pretty simplicity would he then show, trying to amuse us like children with toys; and what an engaging nervousness of manner, as fearing that his efforts might not succeed! Truly he made us all feel like children, and like children embarrassed, but at the same time filled with sympathy for the conscientious, troubled elder-boy who was working so hard to entertain us. A theorist has held the view that there is no feature in man so tell-tale as his spectacles; that the mouth may be compressed and the brow smoothed artificially, but the sheen of the barnacles is diagnostic. And truly it must have been thus with Kelland; for as I still fancy I behold him frisking actively about the platform, pointer in hand, that which I seem to see most clearly is the way his glasses glittered with affection. I never knew but one other man who had (if you will permit the phrase) so kind a spectacle; and that was Dr. Appleton. But the light in his case was tempered and passive; in Kelland's it danced, and changed, and flashed vivaciously among the students, like a perpetual challenge to goodwill.

I cannot say so much about Professor Blackie, for a good reason. Kelland's class I attended, once even gained there a certificate of merit, the only distinction of my University career. But although I am the holder of a certificate of attendance in the professor's own hand, I cannot remember to have been present in the Greek class above a dozen times. Professor Blackie was even kind enough to remark (more than once) while in the very act of writing the document above referred to, that he did not know my face. Indeed, I denied myself many opportunities; acting upon an extensive and highly rational system of truantry, which cost me a great deal of trouble to put in exercise—perhaps as much as would have taught me Greek—and sent me forth into the world and the profession of letters with the merest shadow of an education. But they say it is always a good thing to have taken pains, and that success is its own reward, whatever be its nature; so that, perhaps, even upon this I should plume myself, that no one ever played the truant with more deliberate care, and none ever had more certificates for less education. One consequence, however, of my system is that I have much less to say of Professor Blackie than I had of Professor Kelland; and as he is still alive, and will long, I hope, continue to be so, it will not surprise you very much that I have no intention of saying it.

Meanwhile, how many others have gone—Jenkin, Hodgson, and I know not who besides; and of that tide of students that used to throng the arch and blacken the quadrangle, how many are scattered into the remotest parts of the earth, and how many more have lain down beside their fathers in their "resting-graves"! And again, how many of these last have not found their way there, all too early, through the stress of education! That was one thing, at least, from which my truantry protected me. I am sorry indeed that I have no Greek, but I should be sorrier still if I were dead; nor do I know the name of that branch of knowledge which is worth acquiring at the price of a brain fever. There are many sordid tragedies in the life of the student, above all if he be poor, or drunken, or both; but nothing more moves a wise man's pity than the case of the lad who is in too much hurry to be learned. And so, for the sake of a moral at the end, I will call up one more figure, and have done. A student, ambitious of success by that hot, intemperate manner of study that now grows so common, read night and day for an examination. As he went on, the task became more easy to him, sleep was more easily banished, his brain grew hot and clear and more capacious, the necessary knowledge daily fuller and more orderly. It came to the eve of the trial and he watched all night in his high chamber, reviewing what he knew, and already secure of success. His window looked eastward, and being (as I said) high up, and the house itself standing on a hill, commanded a view over dwindling suburbs to a country horizon. At last my student drew up his blind, and still in quite a jocund humour, looked abroad. Day was breaking, the east was tinging with strange fires, the clouds breaking up for the coming of the sun; and at the sight, nameless terror seized upon his mind. He was sane, his senses were undisturbed; he saw clearly, and knew what he was seeing, and knew that it was normal; but he could neither bear to see it nor find the strength to look away, and fled in panic from his chamber into the enclosure of the street. In the cool air and silence, and among the sleeping houses, his strength was renewed. Nothing troubled him but the memory of what had passed, and an abject fear of its return.

> "Gallo canente, spes redit,
> Aegris salus refunditur,
> Lapsis fides revertitur,"

as they sang of old in Portugal in the Morning Office. But to him that good hour of cockcrow, and the changes of the dawn, had brought panic, and lasting doubt, and such terror as he still shook to think of. He dared not return to his lodging; he could not eat; he sat down, he rose up, he wandered; the city woke about him with its cheerful bustle, the sun climbed overhead; and still he grew but the more absorbed in the distress of his recollection and the fear of his past fear. At the appointed hour, he came to the door of the place of examination; but when he was asked, he had forgotten his name. Seeing him so disordered, they had not the heart to send him away, but gave him a paper and admitted him, still nameless, to the Hall. Vain kindness, vain efforts. He could only sit in a still growing horror, writing nothing, ignorant of all, his mind filled with a single memory of the breaking day and his own intolerable fear. And that same night he was tossing in a brain fever.

People are afraid of war and wounds and dentists, all with excellent reason; but these are not to be compared with such chaotic terrors of the mind as fell on this young man, and made him cover his eyes from the innocent morning. We all have by our bedsides the box of the Merchant Abudah, thank God, securely enough shut; but when a young man sacrifices sleep to labour, let him have a care, for he is playing with the lock.

III

Old Mortality

I

THERE is a certain graveyard, looked upon on the one side by a prison, on the other by the windows of a quiet hotel; below, under a steep cliff, it beholds the traffic of many lines of rail, and the scream of the engine and the shock of meeting buffers mount to it all day long. The aisles are lined with the inclosed sepulchres of families, door beyond door, like houses in a street; and in the morning the shadow of the prison turrets, and of many tall memorials, fall upon the graves. There, in the hot fits of youth, I came to be unhappy. Pleasant incidents are woven with my memory of the place. I here made friends with a certain plain old gentleman, a visitor on sunny mornings, gravely cheerful, who, with one eye upon the place that awaited him, chirped about his youth like winter sparrows; a beautiful housemaid of the hotel once, for some days together, dumbly flirted with me from a window and kept my wild heart flying; and once—she possibly remembers—the wise Eugenia followed me to that austere inclosure. Her hair came down, and in the shelter of the tomb my trembling fingers helped her to repair the braid. But for the most part I went there solitary and, with irrevocable emotion, pored on the names of the forgotten. Name after name, and to each the conventional attributions and the idle dates: a regiment of the unknown that had been the joy of mothers, and had thrilled with the illusions of youth, and at last, in the dim sick-room, wrestled with the pangs of old mortality. In that whole crew of the silenced there was but one of whom my fancy had received a picture; and he, with his comely, florid countenance, bewigged and habited in scarlet, and in his day combining fame and popularity, stood forth, like a taunt, among that company of phantom appellations. It was then possible to leave behind us something more explicit than these severe, monotonous and lying epitaphs; and the thing left, the memory of a painted picture and what we call the immortality of a name, was hardly more desirable than mere oblivion. Even David Hume, as he lay composed beneath that "circular idea," was fainter than a dream; and when the housemaid, broom in hand, smiled and beckoned from the open window, the fame of that bewigged philosopher melted like a raindrop in the sea.

And yet in soberness I cared as little for the housemaid as for David Hume. The interests of youth are rarely frank; his passions, like Noah's dove, come home to roost. The fire, sensibility, and volume of his own nature, that is all that he has learned to recognise. The tumultuary and gray tide of life, the empire of routine, the unrejoicing faces of his elders, fill him with contemptuous surprise; there also he seems to walk among the tombs of spirits; and it is only in the course of years, and after much rubbing with his fellow-men, that he begins by glimpses to see himself from without and his fellows from within: to know his own for one among the thousand undenoted countenances of the city street, and to divine in others the throb of human agony and hope. In the meantime he will avoid the hospital doors, the pale faces, the cripple, the sweet whiff of chloroform—for there, on the most thoughtless, the pains of others are burned home; but he will continue to walk, in a divine self-pity, the aisles of the forgotten graveyard. The length of man's life, which is endless to the brave and busy, is scorned by his ambitious thought. He cannot bear to have come for so little, and to go again so wholly. He cannot bear, above all, in that brief scene, to be still idle, and by way of cure, neglects the little that he has to do. The parable of the talent is the brief epitome of youth. To believe in immortality is one thing, but it is first needful to believe in life. Denunciatory preachers seem not to suspect that they may be taken gravely and in evil part; that young men may come to think of time as of a moment, and with the pride of Satan wave back the inadequate gift. Yet here is a true peril; this it is that sets them to pace the graveyard alleys and to read, with strange extremes of pity and derision, the memorials of the dead.

Books were the proper remedy: books of vivid human import, forcing upon their minds the issues, pleasures, busyness, importance and immediacy of that life in which they stand; books of smiling or heroic temper, to excite or to console; books of a large design, shadowing the complexity of that game of consequences to which we all sit down, the hanger-back not least. But the average sermon flees the point, disporting itself in that eternity of which we know, and need to know, so little; avoiding the bright, crowded and momentous fields of life where destiny awaits us. Upon the average book a writer may be silent; he may set it down to his ill-hap that when his own youth was in the acrid fermentation he should have fallen and fed upon the cheerless fields of Obermann. Yet to Mr. Arnold who led him to these pastures, he still bears a grudge. The day is perhaps not far off when people will begin to count *Moll Flanders*, ay, or *The Country Wife*, more wholesome and more pious diet than these guide-books to consistent egoism.

But the most inhuman of boys soon wearies of the inhumanity of Obermann. And even while I still continued to be a haunter of the graveyard, I began insensibly to turn my attention to the grave-diggers, and was weaned out of myself to observe the conduct of visitors. This was day-spring, indeed, to a lad in such great darkness. Not that I began to see men, or to try to see them, from within, nor to learn charity and modesty and justice from the sight; but still stared at them externally from the prison windows of my affectation. Once I remember to have observed two working-women with a baby halting by a grave; there was something monumental in the grouping, one upright carrying the child, the other with bowed face crouching by her side. A wreath of immortelles under a glass dome had thus attracted them; and, drawing near, I overheard their judgment on that wonder. "Eh! what extravagance!" To a youth afflicted with the callosity of sentiment, this quaint and pregnant saying appeared merely base.

My acquaintance with grave-diggers, considering its length, was unremarkable. One, indeed, whom I found plying his spade in the red evening, high above Allan Water and in the shadow of Dunblane Cathedral, told me of his acquaintance with the birds that still attended on his labours; how some would even perch about him, waiting for their prey; and in a true Sexton's Calendar, how the species varied with the season of the year. But this was the very poetry of the profession. The others whom I knew were somewhat dry. A faint flavour of the gardener hung about them, but sophisticated and disbloomed. They had engagements to keep, not alone with the deliberate series of the seasons, but with mankind's clocks and hour-long measurement of time. And thus there was no leisure for the relishing pinch, or the hour-long gossip, foot on spade. They were men wrapped up in their grim business; they liked well to open long-closed family vaults, blowing in the key and throwing wide the grating; and they carried in their minds a calendar of names and dates. It would be "in fifty-twa" that such a tomb was last opened for "Miss Jemimy." It was thus they spoke of their past patients—familiarly but not without respect, like old family servants. Here is indeed a servant, whom we forget that we possess; who does not wait at the bright table, or run at the bell's summons, but patiently smokes his pipe beside the mortuary fire, and in his faithful memory notches the burials of our race. To suspect Shakespeare in his maturity of a superficial touch savours of paradox; yet he was surely in error when he attributed insensibility to the digger of the grave. But perhaps it is on Hamlet that the charge should lie; or perhaps the English sexton differs from the Scotch. The "goodman delver," reckoning up his years of office, might have at least suggested other thoughts. It is a pride common among sextons. A cabinet-maker does not count his cabinets, nor even an author his volumes, save when they stare upon him from the shelves; but the grave-digger numbers his graves. He would indeed be something different from human if his solitary open-air and tragic labours left not a broad mark upon his mind. There, in his tranquil aisle, apart from city clamour, among the cats and robins and the ancient effigies and legends of the tomb, he waits the continual passage of his contemporaries, falling like minute drops into eternity. As they fall, he counts them; and this enumeration, which was at first perhaps appalling to his soul, in the process of years and by the kindly influence of habit grows to be his pride and pleasure. There are many common stories telling how he piques himself on crowded cemeteries. But I will rather tell of the old grave-digger of Monkton, to whose unsuffering bedside the minister was summoned. He dwelt in a cottage built into the wall of the churchyard; and through a bull's-eye pane above his bed he could see, as he lay dying, the rank grasses and the upright and recumbent stones. Dr. Laurie was, I think, a Moderate: 'tis certain, at least, that he took a very Roman view of deathbed dispositions; for he told the old man that he had lived beyond man's natural years, that his life had been easy and reputable, that his family had all grown up and been a credit to his care, and that it now behoved him unregretfully to gird his loins and follow the majority. The grave-digger heard him out; then he raised himself upon one elbow, and with the other hand pointed through the window to the scene of his life-long labours. "Doctor," he said, "I ha'e laid three hunner and fower-score in that kirk-yaird; an' it had been His wull," indicating

Heaven, "I would ha'e likit weel to ha'e made out the fower hunner." But it was not to be; this tragedian of the fifth act had now another part to play; and the time had come when others were to gird and carry him.

II

I would fain strike a note that should be more heroical; but the ground of all youth's suffering, solitude, hysteria, and haunting of the grave, is nothing else than naked, ignorant selfishness. It is himself that he sees dead; those are his virtues that are forgotten; his is the vague epitaph. Pity him but the more, if pity be your cue; for where a man is all pride, vanity, and personal aspiration, he goes through fire unshielded. In every part and corner of our life, to lose oneself is to be gainer; to forget oneself is to be happy; and this poor, laughable and tragic fool has not yet learned the rudiments; himself, giant Prometheus, is still ironed on the peaks of Caucasus. But by-and-by his truant interests will leave that tortured body, slip abroad and gather flowers. Then shall death appear before him in an altered guise; no longer as a doom peculiar to himself, whether fate's crowning injustice or his own last vengeance upon those who fail to value him; but now as a power that wounds him far more tenderly, not without solemn compensations, taking and giving, bereaving and yet storing up.

The first step for all is to learn to the dregs our own ignoble fallibility. When we have fallen through storey after storey of our vanity and aspiration, and sit rueful among the ruins, then it is that we begin to measure the stature of our friends: how they stand between us and our own contempt, believing in our best; how, linking us with others, and still spreading wide the influential circle, they weave us in and in with the fabric of contemporary life; and to what petty size they dwarf the virtues and the vices that appeared gigantic in our youth. So that at the last, when such a pin falls out—when there vanishes in the least breath of time one of those rich magazines of life on which we draw for our supply—when he who had first dawned upon us as a face among the faces of the city, and, still growing, came to bulk on our regard with those clear features of the loved and living man, falls in a breath to memory and shadow, there falls along with him a whole wing of the palace of our life.

III

One such face I now remember; one such blank some half a dozen of us labour to dissemble. In his youth he was most beautiful in person, most serene and genial by disposition; full of racy words and quaint thoughts. Laughter attended on his coming. He had the air of a great gentleman, jovial and royal with his equals, and to the poorest student gentle and attentive. Power seemed to reside in him exhaustless; we saw him stoop to play with us, but held him marked for higher destinies; we loved his notice; and I have rarely had my pride more gratified than when he sat at my father's table my acknowledged friend. So he walked among us, both hands full of gifts, carrying with nonchalance the seeds of a most influential life.

The powers and the ground of friendship is a mystery; but, looking back, I can discern that, in part, we loved the thing he was, for some shadow of what he was to be. For with all his beauty, power, breeding, urbanity and mirth, there was in those days something soulless in our friend. He would astonish us by sallies, witty, innocent and inhumane; and by a misapplied Johnsonian pleasantry, demolish honest sentiment. I can still see and hear him, as he went his way along the lamplit streets, *Là ci darem la mano* on his lips, a noble figure of a youth, but following vanity and incredulous of good; and sure enough, somewhere on the high seas of life, with his health, his hopes, his patrimony and his self-respect, miserably went down.

From this disaster, like a spent swimmer, he came desperately ashore, bankrupt of money and consideration; creeping to the family he had deserted; with broken wing, never more to rise. But in his face there was a light of knowledge that was new to it. Of the wounds of his body he was never healed; died of them gradually, with clear-eyed resignation; of his wounded pride, we knew only from his silence. He returned to that city where he had lorded it in his ambitious youth; lived there alone, seeing few; striving to retrieve the irretrievable; at times still grappling with that mortal frailty that had brought him down; still joying in his friend's successes; his laugh still ready but with kindlier music; and over all his thoughts the shadow of that unalterable law which he had disavowed and which had brought him low. Lastly, when his bodily evils had quite disabled him, he lay a great while dying, still without complaint, still finding interests; to his last step gentle, urbane and with the will to smile.

The tale of this great failure is, to those who remained true to him, the tale of a success. In his youth he took thought for no one but himself; when he came ashore again, his whole armada lost, he seemed to think of none but others. Such was his tenderness for others, such his instinct of fine courtesy and pride, that of that impure passion of remorse he never breathed a syllable; even regret was rare with him, and pointed with a jest. You would not have dreamed, if you had known him then, that this was that great failure, that beacon to young men, over whose fall a whole society had hissed and pointed fingers. Often have we gone to him, red-hot with our own hopeful sorrows, railing on the rose-leaves in our princely bed of life, and he would patiently give ear and wisely counsel; and it was only upon some return of our own thoughts that we were reminded what manner of man this was to whom we disembosomed: a man, by his own fault, ruined; shut out of the garden of his gifts; his whole city of hope both ploughed and salted; silently awaiting the deliverer. Then something took us by the throat; and to see him there, so gentle, patient, brave and pious, oppressed but not cast down, sorrow was so swallowed up in admiration that we could not dare to pity him. Even if the old fault flashed out again, it but awoke our wonder that, in that lost battle, he should still have the energy to fight. He had gone to ruin with a kind of kingly *abandon*, like one who condescended; but once ruined, with the lights all out, he fought as for a kingdom. Most men, finding themselves the authors of their own disgrace, rail the louder against God or destiny. Most men, when they repent, oblige their friends to share the bitterness of that repentance. But he had held an inquest and passed sentence: *mene, mene;* and condemned himself to smiling silence. He had given trouble enough; had earned misfortune amply, and foregone the right to murmur.

Thus was our old comrade, like Samson, careless in his days of strength; but on the coming of adversity, and when that strength was gone that had betrayed him—“for our strength is weakness"—he began to blossom and bring forth. Well, now, he is out of the fight: the burden that he bore thrown down before the great deliverer. We

> "in the vast cathedral leave him;
> God accept him,
> Christ receive him!"

IV

If we go now and look on these innumerable epitaphs, the pathos and the irony are strangely fled. They do not stand merely to the dead, these foolish monuments; they are pillars and legends set up to glorify the difficult but not desperate life of man. This ground is hallowed by the heroes of defeat.

I see the indifferent pass before my friend's last resting-place; pause, with a shrug of pity, marvelling that so rich an argosy had sunk. A pity, now that he is done with suffering, a pity most uncalled for, and an ignorant wonder. Before those who loved him, his memory shines like a reproach; they honour him for silent lessons; they cherish his example; and in what remains before them of their toil, fear to be unworthy of the dead. For this proud man was one of those who prospered in the valley of humiliation;—of whom Bunyan wrote that, "Though

Christian had the hard hap to meet in the valley with Apollyon, yet I must tell you, that in former times men have met with angels here; have found pearls here; and have in this place found the words of life."

IV

A College Magazine

I

ALL through my boyhood and youth, I was known and pointed out for the pattern of an idler; and yet I was always busy on my own private end, which was to learn to write. I kept always two books in my pocket, one to read, one to write in. As I walked, my mind was busy fitting what I saw with appropriate words; when I sat by the roadside, I would either read, or a pencil and a penny version-book would be in my hand, to note down the features of the scene or commemorate some halting stanzas. Thus I lived with words. And what I thus wrote was for no ulterior use, it was written consciously for practice. It was not so much that I wished to be an author (though I wished that too) as that I had vowed that I would learn to write. That was a proficiency that tempted me; and I practised to acquire it, as men learn to whittle, in a wager with myself. Description was the principal field of my exercise; for to anyone with senses there is always something worth describing, and town and country are but one continuous subject. But I worked in other ways also; often accompanied my walks with dramatic dialogues, in which I played many parts; and often exercised myself in writing down conversations from memory.

This was all excellent, no doubt; so were the diaries I sometimes tried to keep, but always and very speedily discarded, finding them a school of posturing and melancholy self-deception. And yet this was not the most efficient part of my training. Good though it was, it only taught me (so far as I have learned them at all) the lower and less intellectual elements of the art, the choice of the essential note and the right word: things that to a happier constitution had perhaps come by nature. And regarded as training, it had one grave defect; for it set me no standard of achievement. So that there was perhaps more profit, as there was certainly more effort, in my secret labours at home. Whenever I read a book or a passage that particularly pleased me, in which a thing was said or an effect rendered with propriety, in which there was either some conspicuous force or some happy distinction in the style, I must sit down at once and set myself to ape that quality. I was unsuccessful, and I knew it; and tried again, and was again unsuccessful and always unsuccessful; but at least in these vain bouts, I got some practice in rhythm, in harmony, in construction and the co-ordination of parts. I have thus played the sedulous ape to Hazlitt, to Lamb, to Wordsworth, to Sir Thomas Browne, to Defoe, to Hawthorne, to Montaigne, to Baudelaire and to Obermann. I remember one of these monkey tricks, which was called *The Vanity of Morals:* it was to have had a second part, *The Vanity of Knowledge;* and as I had neither morality nor scholarship, the names were apt; but the second part was never attempted, and the first part was written (which is my reason for recalling it, ghost-like, from its ashes) no less than three times: first in the manner of Hazlitt, second in the manner of Ruskin, who had cast on me a passing spell, and third, in a laborious pasticcio of Sir Thomas Browne. So with my other works: *Cain,* an epic, was (save the mark!) an imitation of *Sordello: Robin Hood,* a tale in verse, took an eclectic middle course among the fields of Keats, Chaucer and Morris: in *Monmouth,* a tragedy, I reclined on the bosom of Mr. Swinburne; in my innumerable gouty-footed lyrics, I followed many masters; in the first draft of *The King's Pardon,* a tragedy, I was on the trail of no lesser man than John Webster; in the second draft of the same piece, with staggering versatility, I had shifted my allegiance to Congreve, and of course conceived my fable in a less serious vein—for it was not Congreve's verse, it was his exquisite prose, that I admired and sought to copy. Even at the age of thirteen I had tried to do justice to the inhabitants of the famous city of Peebles in the style of the *Book of Snobs.* So I might go on for ever, through all my abortive novels, and down to my later plays, of which I think more tenderly, for they were not only conceived at first under the bracing influence of old Dumas, but have met with resurrection; one, strangely bettered by another hand, came on the stage itself and was played by bodily actors; the other, originally known as *Semiramis: a Tragedy*, I have observed on bookstalls under the *alias* of *Prince Otto*. But enough has been said to show by what arts of impersonation, and in what purely ventriloquial efforts I first saw my words on paper.

That, like it or not, is the way to learn to write; whether I have profited or not, that is the way. It was so Keats learned, and there was never a finer temperament for literature than Keats's; it was so, if we could trace it out, that all men have learned; and that is why a revival of letters is always accompanied or heralded by a cast back to earlier and fresher models. Perhaps I hear someone cry out: But this is not the way to be original! It is not; nor is there any way but to be born so. Nor yet, if you are born original, is there anything in this training that shall clip the wings of your originality. There can be none more original than Montaigne, neither could any be more unlike Cicero; yet no craftsman can fail to see how much the one must have tried in his time to imitate the other. Burns is the very type of a prime force in letters: he was of all men the most imitative. Shakespeare himself, the imperial, proceeds directly from a school. It is only from a school that we can expect to have good writers; it is almost invariably from a school that great writers, these lawless exceptions, issue. Nor is there anything here that should astonish the considerate. Before he can tell what cadences he truly prefers, the student should have tried all that are possible; before he can choose and preserve a fitting key of words, he should long have practised the literary scales; and it is only after years of such gymnastic that he can sit down at last, legions of words swarming to his call, dozens of turns of phrase simultaneously bidding for his choice, and he himself knowing what he wants to do and (within the narrow limit of a man's ability) able to do it.

And it is the great point of these imitations that there still shines beyond the student's reach his inimitable model. Let him try as he please, he is still sure of failure; and it is a very old and a very true saying that failure is the only highroad to success. I must have had some disposition to learn; for I clear-sightedly condemned my own performances. I liked doing them indeed; but when they were done, I could see they were rubbish. In consequence, I very rarely showed them even to my friends; and such friends as I chose to be my confidants I must have chosen well, for they had the friendliness to be quite plain with me. "Padding," said one. Another wrote: "I cannot understand why you do lyrics so badly." No more could I! Thrice I put myself in the way of a more authoritative rebuff, by sending a paper to a magazine. These were returned; and I was not surprised nor even pained. If they had not been looked at, as (like all amateurs) I suspected was the case, there was no good in repeating the experiment; if they had been looked at—well, then I had not yet learned to write, and I must keep on learning and living. Lastly, I had a piece of good fortune which is the occasion of this paper, and by which I was able to see my literature in print, and to measure experimentally how far I stood from the favour of the public.

II

The Speculative Society is a body of some antiquity, and has counted among its members Scott, Brougham, Jeffrey, Horner, Benjamin Constant, Robert Emmet, and many a legal and local celebrity besides. By an accident, variously explained, it has its rooms in the very buildings of the University of Edinburgh: a hall, Turkey-carpeted, hung with pictures, looking, when lighted up at night with fire and candle, like some goodly dining-room; a passage-like library, walled with books in their wire cages; and a corridor with a fireplace, benches, a table, many prints of famous members, and a mural tablet to the virtues of a former secretary. Here a member can warm himself and loaf and read; here, in defiance of Senatus-consults, he can smoke. The Senatus looks askance at these privileges; looks even with a somewhat vinegar aspect on the whole society; which argues a lack of proportion in the learned mind, for the world, we may be sure, will prize far higher this haunt of dead lions than all the living dogs of the professorate.

I sat one December morning in the library of the Speculative; a very humble-minded youth, though it was a virtue I never had much credit for; yet proud of my privileges as a member of the Spec.; proud of the pipe I was smoking in the teeth of the Senatus; and in particular, proud of being in the next room to three very distinguished students, who were then conversing beside the corridor fire. One of these has now his name on the back of several volumes, and his voice, I learn, is influential in the law courts. Of the death of the second, you have just been reading what I had to say. And the third also has escaped out of that battle of life in which he fought so hard, it may be so unwisely. They were all three, as I have said, notable students; but this was the most conspicuous. Wealthy, handsome, ambitious, adventurous, diplomatic, a reader of Balzac, and of all men that I have known, the most like to one of Balzac's characters, he led a life, and was attended by an ill fortune, that could be properly set forth only in the *Comédie Humaine*. He had then his eye on Parliament; and soon after the time of which I write, he made a showy speech at a political dinner, was cried up to heaven next day in the *Courant*, and the day after was dashed lower than earth with a charge of plagiarism in the *Scotsman*. Report would have it (I daresay, very wrongly) that he was betrayed by one in whom he particularly trusted, and that the author of the charge had learned its truth from his own lips. Thus, at least, he was up one day on a pinnacle, admired and envied by all; and the next, though still but a boy, he was publicly disgraced. The blow would have broken a less finely tempered spirit; and even him I suppose it rendered reckless; for he took flight to London, and there, in a fast club, disposed of the bulk of his considerable patrimony in the space of one winter. For years thereafter he lived I know not how; always well dressed, always in good hotels and good society, always with empty pockets. The charm of his manner may have stood him in good stead; but though my own manners are very agreeable, I have never found in them a source of livelihood; and to explain the miracle of his continued existence, I must fall back upon the theory of the philosopher, that in his case, as in all of the same kind, "there was a suffering relative in the background." From this genteel eclipse he reappeared upon the scene, and presently sought me out in the character of a generous editor. It is in this part that I best remember him; tall, slender, with a not ungraceful stoop; looking quite like a refined gentleman, and quite like an urbane adventurer; smiling with an engaging ambiguity; cocking at you one peaked eyebrow with a great appearance of finesse; speaking low and sweet and thick, with a touch of burr; telling strange tales with singular deliberation and, to a patient listener, excellent effect. After all these ups and downs, he seemed still, like the rich student that he was of yore, to breathe of money; seemed still perfectly sure of himself and certain of his end. Yet he was then upon the brink of his last overthrow. He had set himself to found the strangest thing in our society: one of those periodical sheets from which men suppose themselves to learn opinions; in which young gentlemen from the universities are encouraged, at so much a line, to garble facts, insult foreign nations and calumniate private individuals; and which are now the source of glory, so that if a man's name be often enough printed there, he becomes a kind of demigod; and people will pardon him when he talks back and forth, as they do for Mr. Gladstone; and crowd him to suffocation on railway platforms, as they did the other day to General Boulanger; and buy his literary works, as I hope you have just done for me. Our fathers, when they were upon some great enterprise, would sacrifice a life; building, it may be, a favourite slave into the foundations of their palace. It was with his own life that my companion disarmed the envy of the gods. He fought his paper single-handed; trusting no one, for he was something of a cynic; up early and down late, for he was nothing of a sluggard; daily ear-wigging influential men, for he was a master of ingratiation. In that slender and silken fellow there must have been a rare vein of courage, that he should thus have died at his employment; and doubtless ambition spoke loudly in his ear, and doubtless love also, for it seems there was a marriage in his view had he succeeded. But he died, and his paper died after him; and of all this grace, and tact, and courage, it must seem to our blind eyes as if there had come literally nothing.

These three students sat, as I was saying, in the corridor, under the mural tablet that records the virtues of Macbean, the former secretary. We would often smile at that ineloquent memorial, and thought it a poor thing to come into the world at all and have no more behind one than Macbean. And yet of these three, two are gone and have left less; and this book, perhaps, when it is old and foxy, and someone picks it up in a corner of a book-shop, and glances through it, smiling at the old, graceless turns of speech, and perhaps for the love of *Alma Mater* (which may be still extant and flourishing) buys it, not without haggling, for some pence—this book may alone preserve a memory of James Walter Ferrier and Robert Glasgow Brown.

Their thoughts ran very differently on that

December morning; they were all on fire with ambition; and when they had called me in to them, and made me a sharer in their design, I too became drunken with pride and hope. We were to found a University magazine. A pair of little, active brothers—Livingstone by name, great skippers on the foot, great rubbers of the hands, who kept a book-shop over against the University building—had been debauched to play the part of publishers. We four were to be conjunct editors and, what was the main point of the concern, to print our own works; while, by every rule of arithmetic—that flatterer of credulity—the adventure must succeed and bring great profit. Well, well: it was a bright vision. I went home that morning walking upon air. To have been chosen by these three distinguished students was to me the most unspeakable advance; it was my first draught of consideration; it reconciled me to myself and to my fellow-men; and as I steered round the railings at the Tron, I could not withhold my lips from smiling publicly. Yet, in the bottom of my heart, I knew that magazine would be a grim fiasco; I knew it would not be worth reading; I knew, even if it were, that nobody would read it; and I kept wondering how I should be able, upon my compact income of twelve pounds per annum, payable monthly, to meet my share in the expense. It was a comfortable thought to me that I had a father.

The magazine appeared, in a yellow cover,

which was the best part of it, for at least it was unassuming; it ran four months in undisturbed obscurity, and died without a gasp. The first number was edited by all four of us with prodigious bustle; the second fell principally into the hands of Ferrier and me; the third I edited alone; and it has long been a solemn question who it was that edited the fourth. It would perhaps be still more difficult to say who read it. Poor yellow sheet, that looked so hopefully in the Livingstones' window! Poor, harmless paper, that might have gone to print a *Shakespeare* on, and was instead so clumsily defaced with nonsense! And, shall I say, Poor Editors? I cannot pity myself, to whom it was all pure gain. It was no news to me, but only the wholesome confirmation of my judgment, when the magazine struggled into half-birth, and instantly sickened and subsided into night. I had sent a copy to the lady with whom my heart was at that time somewhat engaged, and who did all that in her lay to break it; and she, with some tact, passed over the gift and my cherished contributions in silence. I will not say that I was pleased at this; but I will tell her now, if by any chance she takes up the work of her former servant, that I thought the better of her taste. I cleared the decks after this lost engagement; had the necessary interview with my father, which passed off not amiss; paid over my share of the expense to the two little, active brothers, who rubbed their hands as much, but methought skipped rather less than formerly, having perhaps, these two also, embarked upon the enterprise with some graceful illusions; and then, reviewing the whole episode, I told myself that the time was not yet ripe, nor the man ready; and to work I went again with my penny version-books, having fallen back in one day from the printed author to the manuscript student.

III

From this defunct periodical I am going to reprint one of my own papers. The poor little piece is all tail-foremost. I have done my best to straighten its array, I have pruned it fearlessly, and it remains invertebrate and wordy. No self-respecting magazine would print the thing; and here you behold it in a bound volume, not for any worth of its own, but for the sake of the man whom it purports dimly to represent and some of whose sayings it preserves; so that in this volume of Memories and Portraits, Robert Young, the Swanston gardener, may stand alongside of John Todd, the Swanston shepherd. Not that John and Robert drew very close together in their lives; for John was rough, he smelt of the windy brae; and Robert was gentle, and smacked of the garden in the hollow. Perhaps it is to my shame that I liked John the better of the two; he had grit and dash, and that salt of the Old Adam that pleases men with any savage inheritance of blood; and he was a wayfarer besides, and took my gipsy fancy. But however that may be, and however Robert's profile may be blurred in the boyish sketch that follows, he was a man of a most quaint and beautiful nature, whom, if it were possible to recast a piece of work so old, I should like well to draw again with a maturer touch. And as I think of him and of John, I wonder in what other country two such men would be found dwelling together, in a hamlet of some twenty cottages, in the woody fold of a green hill.

V

An Old Scotch Gardener

I THINK I might almost have said the last: somewhere, indeed, in the uttermost glens of the Lammermuir or among the south-western hills there may yet linger a decrepit representative of this bygone good fellowship; but as far as actual experience goes, I have only met one man in my life who might fitly be quoted in the same breath with Andrew Fairservice,—though without his vices. He was a man whose very presence could impart a savour of quaint antiquity to the baldest and most modern flower-pots. There was a dignity about his tall stooping form, and an earnestness in his wrinkled face that recalled Don Quixote; but a Don Quixote who had come through the training of the Covenant, and been nourished in his youth on *Walker's Lives* and *The Hind Let Loose*.

Now, as I could not bear to let such a man pass away with no sketch preserved of his old-fashioned virtues, I hope the reader will take this as an excuse for the present paper, and judge as kindly as he can the infirmities of my description. To mc, who find it so difficult to tell the little that I know, he stands essentially as a *genius loci*. It is impossible to separate his spare form and old straw hat from the garden in the lap of the hill, with its rocks overgrown with clematis, its shadowy walks, and the splendid breadth of champaign that one saw from the north-west corner. The garden and gardener seem part and parcel of each other. When I take him from his right surroundings and try to make him appear for me on paper, he looks unreal and phantasmal: the best that I can say may convey some notion to those that never saw him, but to me it will be ever impotent.

The first time that I saw him, I fancy Robert was pretty old already: he had certainly begun to use his years as a stalking-horse. Latterly he was beyond all the impudences of logic, considering a reference to the parish register worth all the reasons in the world. "*I am old and well stricken in years*," he was wont to say; and I never found any one bold enough to answer the argument. Apart from this vantage that he kept over all who were not yet octogenarian, he had some other drawbacks as a gardener. He shrank the very place he cultivated. The dignity and reduced gentility of his appearance made the small garden cut a sorry figure. He was full of tales of greater situations in his younger days. He spoke of castles and parks with a humbling familiarity. He told of places where under-gardeners had trembled at his looks, where there were meres and swanneries, labyrinths of walk and wildernesses of sad shrubbery in his control, till you could not help feeling that it was condescension on his part to dress your humbler garden plots. You were thrown at once into an invidious position. You felt that you were profiting by the needs of dignity, and that his poverty and not his will consented to your vulgar rule. Involuntarily you compared yourself with the swineherd that made Alfred watch his cakes, or some bloated citizen who may have given his sons and his condescension to the fallen Dionysius. Nor were the disagreeables purely fanciful and metaphysical, for the sway that he exercised over your feelings he extended to your garden, and, through the garden, to your diet. He would trim a hedge, throw away a favourite plant, or fill the most favoured and fertile section of the garden with a vegetable that none of us could eat, in supreme contempt for our opinion. If you asked him to send you in one of your own artichokes, "*That I wull, mem,*" he would say, "*with pleasure, for it is mair blessed to give than to receive.*" Ay, and even when, by extra twisting of the screw, we prevailed on him to prefer our commands to his own inclination, and he went away, stately and sad, professing that "*our wull was his pleasure,*" but yet reminding us that he would do it "*with feelin's,*"—even then, I say, the triumphant master felt humbled in his triumph, felt that he ruled on sufferance only, that he was taking a mean advantage of the other's low estate, and that the whole scene had been one of those " slights that patient merit of the unworthy takes."

In flowers his taste was old-fashioned and catholic; affecting sunflowers and dahlias, wall-flowers and roses, and holding in supreme aversion whatsoever was fantastic, new-fashioned or wild. There was one exception to this sweeping ban. Foxgloves, though undoubtedly guilty on the last count, he not only spared, but loved; and when the shrubbery was being thinned, he stayed his hand and dexterously manipulated his bill in order to save every stately stem. In boyhood, as he told me once, speaking in that tone that only actors and the old-fashioned common folk can use nowadays, his heart grew "*proud*" within him when he came on a burn-course among the braes of Manor that shone purple with their graceful trophies; and not all his apprenticeship and practice for so many years of precise gardening had banished these boyish recollections from his heart. Indeed, he was a man keenly alive to the beauty of all that was bygone. He abounded in old stories of his boyhood, and kept pious account of all his former pleasures; and when he went (on a holiday) to visit one of the fabled great places of the earth where he had served before, he came back full of little pre-Raphaelite reminiscences that showed real passion for the past, such as might have shaken hands with Hazlitt or Jean-Jacques.

But however his sympathy with his old feelings might affect his liking for the foxgloves, the very truth was that he scorned all flowers together. They were but garnishings, childish toys, trifling ornaments for ladies' chimney-shelves. It was towards his cauliflowers and peas and cabbage that his heart grew warm. His preference for the more useful growths was such that cabbages were found invading the flower-plots, and an outpost of savoys was once discovered in the centre of the lawn. He would prelect over some thriving plant with wonderful enthusiasm, piling reminiscence on reminiscence of former and perhaps yet finer specimens. Yet even then he did not let the credit leave himself. He had, indeed, raised "*finer o' them;*" but it seemed that no one else had been favoured with a like success. All other gardeners, in fact, were mere foils to his own superior attainments; and he would recount, with perfect soberness of voice and visage, how so and so had wondered, and such another could scarcely give credit to his eyes. Nor was it with his rivals only that he parted praise and blame. If you remarked how well a plant was looking, he would gravely touch his hat and thank you with solemn unction; all credit in the matter falling to him. If, on the other hand, you called his attention to some back-going vegetable, he would quote Scripture: "*Paul may plant and Apollos may water;*" all blame being left to Providence, on the score of deficient rain or untimely frosts.

There was one thing in the garden that shared his preference with his favourite cabbages and rhubarb, and that other was the beehive. Their sound, their industry, perhaps their sweet product also, had taken hold of his imagination and heart, whether by way of memory or no I cannot say, although perhaps the bees too were linked to him by some recollection of Manor braes and his country childhood. Nevertheless, he was too chary of his personal safety or (let me rather say) his personal dignity to mingle in any active office towards them. But he could stand by while one of the contemned rivals did the work for him, and protest that it was quite safe in spite of his own considerate distance and the cries of the distressed assistant. In regard to bees, he was rather a man of word than deed, and some of his most striking sentences had the bees for text. "*They are indeed wonderfu' creatures, mem,*" he said once. "*They just mind me o' what the Queen of Sheba said to Solomon—and I think she said it wi' a sigh,—'The half of it hath not been told unto me.'*"

As far as the Bible goes, he was deeply read. Like the old Covenanters, of whom he was the worthy representative, his mouth was full of sacred quotations; it was the book that he had studied most and thought upon most deeply. To many people in his station the Bible, and perhaps Burns, are the only books of any vital literary merit that they read, feeding themselves, for the rest, on the draff of country newspapers, and the very instructive but not very palatable pabulum of some cheap educational series. This was Robert's position. All day long he had dreamed of the Hebrew stories, and his head had been full of Hebrew poetry and Gospel ethics; until they had struck deep root into his heart, and the very expressions had become a part of him; so that he rarely spoke without some antique idiom or Scripture mannerism that gave a raciness to the merest trivialities of talk. But the influence of the Bible did not stop here. There was more in Robert than quaint phrase and ready store of reference. He was imbued with a spirit of peace and love: he interposed between man and wife: he threw himself between the angry, touching his hat the while with all the ceremony of an usher: he protected the birds from everybody but himself, seeing, I suppose, a great difference between official execution and wanton sport. His mistress telling him one day to put some ferns into his master's particular corner, and adding, "Though, indeed, Robert, he doesn't deserve them, for he wouldn't help me to gather them," "*Eh, mem,*" replies Robert, "*but I wouldnae say that, for I think he's just a most deservin' gentleman.*" Again, two of our friends, who were on intimate terms, and accustomed to use language to each other, somewhat without the bounds of the parliamentary, happened to differ about the position of a seat in the garden. The discussion, as was usual when these two were at it, soon waxed tolerably insulting on both sides. Every one accustomed to such controversies several times a day was quietly enjoying this prize-fight of somewhat abusive wit—every one but Robert, to whom the perfect good faith of the whole quarrel seemed unquestionable, and who, after having waited till his conscience would suffer him to wait no more, and till he expected every moment that the disputants would fall to blows, cut suddenly in with tones of almost tearful entreaty: "*Eh, but, gentlemen, I wad hae nae mair words about it!*" One thing was noticeable about Robert's religion: it was neither dogmatic nor sectarian. He never expatiated (at least, in my hearing) on the doctrines of his creed, and he never condemned anybody else. I have no doubt that he held all Roman Catholics, Atheists, and Mahometans as considerably out of it; I don't believe he had any sympathy for Prelacy; and the natural feelings of man must have made him a little sore about Free-Churchism; but at least he never talked about these views, never grew controversially noisy, and never openly aspersed the belief or practice of anybody. Now all this is not generally characteristic of Scotch piety; Scotch sects being churches militant with a vengeance, and Scotch believers perpetual crusaders the one against the other, and missionaries the one to the other. Perhaps Robert's originally tender heart was what made the difference; or, perhaps, his solitary and pleasant labour among fruits and flowers had taught him a more sunshiny creed than those whose work is among the tares of fallen humanity; and the soft influences of the garden had entered deep into his spirit,

> "Annihilating all that's made
> To a green thought in a green shade."

But I could go on for ever chronicling his golden sayings or telling of his innocent and living piety. I had meant to tell of his cottage, with the German pipe hung reverently above the fire, and the shell box that he had made for his son, and of which he would say pathetically: "*He was real pleased wi' it at first, but I think he's got a kind o' tired o' it now*"—the son being then a man of about forty. But I will let all these pass. "'Tis more significant: he's dead." The earth, that he had digged so much in his life, was dug out by another for himself; and the flowers that he had tended drew their life still from him, but in a new and nearer way. A bird flew about the open grave, as if it too wished to honour the obsequies of one who had so often quoted Scripture in favour of its kind: "Are not two sparrows sold for one farthing, and yet not one of them falleth to the ground."

Yes, he is dead. But the kings did not rise in the place of death to greet him "with taunting proverbs" as they rose to greet the haughty Babylonian; for in his life he was lowly, and a peacemaker and a servant of God.

VI

Pastoral

TO leave home in early life is to be stunned and quickened with novelties; but when years have come, it only casts a more endearing light upon the past. As in those composite photographs of Mr. Galton's, the image of each new sitter brings out but the more clearly the central features of the race; when once youth has flown, each new impression only deepens the sense of nationality and the desire of native places. So may some cadet of Royal Écossais or the Albany Regiment, as he mounted guard about French citadels, so may some officer marching his company of the Scots-Dutch among the polders, have felt the soft rains of the Hebrides upon his brow, or started in the ranks at the remembered aroma of peat-smoke. And the rivers of home are dear in particular to all men. This is as old as Naaman, who was jealous for Abana, and Pharpar; it is confined to no race nor country, for I know one of Scottish blood but a child of Suffolk, whose fancy still lingers about the lilied lowland waters of that shire. But the streams of Scotland are incomparable in themselves—or

I am only the more Scottish to suppose so—and their sound and colour dwell for ever in the memory. How often and willingly do I not look again in fancy on Tummel, or Manor, or the talking Airdle, or Dee swirling in its Lynn; on the bright burn of Kinnaird, or the golden burn that pours and sulks in the den behind Kingussie! I think shame to leave out one of these enchantresses, but the list would grow too long if I remembered all; only I may not forget Allan Water, nor birch-wetting Rogie, nor yet Almond; nor, for all its pollutions, that Water of Leith of the many and well-named mills—Bell's Mills, and Canon Mills, and Silver Mills; nor Redford Burn of pleasant memories; nor yet, for all its smallness, that nameless trickle that springs in the green bosom of Allermuir, and is fed from Halkerside with a perennial teacupful, and threads the moss under the Shearer's Knowe, and makes one pool there, overhung by a rock, where I loved to sit and make bad verses, and is then kidnapped in its infancy by subterranean pipes for the service of the sea-beholding city in the plain. From many points in the moss you may see at one glance its whole course and that of all its tributaries; the geographer of this Lilliput may visit all its corners without sitting down, and not yet begin to be breathed; Shearer's Knowe and Halkerside are but names of adjacent cantons on a single shoulder of a hill, as names are squandered (it would seem to the inexpert, in superfluity) upon these upland sheepwalks; a bucket would receive the whole discharge of the toy river; it would take it an appreciable time to fill your morning bath; for the most part, besides, it soaks unseen through the moss; and yet for the sake of auld lang syne, and the figure of a certain *genius loci*, I am condemned to linger awhile in fancy by its shores; and if the nymph (who cannot be above a span in stature) will but inspire my pen, I would gladly carry the reader along with me.

John Todd, when I knew him, was already "the oldest herd on the Pentlands," and had been all his days faithful to that curlew-scattering, sheep-collecting life. He remembered the droving days, when the drove roads, that now lie green and solitary through the heather, were thronged thoroughfares. He had himself often marched flocks into England, sleeping on the hillsides with his caravan; and by his account it was a rough business not without danger. The drove roads lay apart from habitation; the drovers met in the wilderness, as to-day the deep-sea fishers meet off the banks in the solitude of the Atlantic; and in the one as in the other case rough habits and fist-law were the rule. Crimes were committed, sheep filched, and drovers robbed and beaten; most of which offences had a moorland burial and were never heard of in the courts of justice. John, in those days, was at least once attacked,—by two men after his watch,—and at least once, betrayed by his habitual anger, fell under the danger of the law and was clapped into some rustic prison-house, the doors of which he burst in the night and was no more heard of in that quarter. When I knew him, his life had fallen in quieter places, and he had no cares beyond the dulness of his dogs and the inroads of pedestrians from town. But for a man of his propensity to wrath these were enough; he knew neither rest nor peace, except by snatches; in the gray of the summer morning, and already from far up the hill, he would wake the "toun" with the sound of his shoutings; and in the lambing time, his cries were not yet silenced late at night. This wrathful voice of a man unseen might be said to haunt that quarter of the Pentlands, an audible bogie; and no doubt it added to the fear in which men stood of John a touch of something legendary. For my own part, he was at first my enemy, and I, in my character of a rambling boy, his natural abhorrence. It was long before I saw him near at hand, knowing him only by some sudden blast of bellowing from far above, bidding me "c'way oot amang the sheep." The quietest recesses of the hill harboured this ogre; I skulked in my favourite wilderness like a Cameronian of the Killing Time, and John Todd was my Claverhouse, and his dogs my questing dragoons. Little by little we dropped into civilities; his hail at sight of me began to have less of the ring of a war-slogan; soon, we never met but he produced his snuff-box, which was with him, like the calumet with the Red Indian, a part of the heraldry of peace; and at length, in the ripeness of time, we grew to be a pair of friends, and when I lived alone in these parts in the winter, it was a settled thing for John to "give me a cry" over the garden wall as he set forth upon his evening round, and for me to overtake and bear him company.

That dread voice of his that shook the hills when he was angry, fell in ordinary talk very pleasantly upon the ear, with a kind of honied, friendly whine, not far off singing, that was eminently Scottish. He laughed not very often, and when he did, with a sudden, loud haw-haw, hearty but somehow joyless, like an echo from a rock. His face was permanently set and coloured; ruddy and stiff with weathering; more like a picture than a face; yet with a certain strain and a threat of latent anger in the expression, like that of a man trained too fine and harassed with perpetual vigilance. He spoke in the richest dialect of Scotch I ever heard; the words in themselves were a pleasure and often a surprise to me, so that I often came back from one of our patrols with new acquisitions; and this vocabulary he would handle like a master, stalking a little before me, "beard on shoulder," the plaid hanging loosely about him, the yellow staff clapped under his arm, and guiding me uphill by that devious, tactical ascent which seems peculiar to men of his trade. I might count him with the best talkers; only that talking Scotch and talking English seem incomparable acts. He touched on nothing at least, but he adorned it; when he narrated, the scene was before you; when he spoke (as he did mostly) of his own antique business, the thing took on a colour of romance and curiosity that was surprising. The clans of sheep with their particular territories on the hill, and how, in the yearly killings and purchases, each must be proportionally thinned and strengthened; the midnight busyness of animals, the signs of the weather, the cares of the snowy season, the exquisite stupidity of sheep, the exquisite cunning of dogs: all these he could present so humanly, and with so much old experience and living gusto, that weariness was excluded. And in the midst he would suddenly straighten his bowed back, the stick would fly abroad in demonstration, and the sharp thunder of his voice roll out a long itinerary for the dogs, so that you saw at last the use of that great wealth of names for every knowe and howe upon the hillside; and the dogs, having hearkened with lowered tails and raised faces, would run up their flags again to the masthead and spread themselves upon the indicated circuit. It used to fill me with wonder how they could follow and retain so long a story. But John denied these creatures all intelligence; they were the constant butt of his passion and contempt; it was just possible to work with the like of them, he said,—not more than possible. And then he would expand upon the subject of the really good dogs that he had known, and the one really good dog that he had himself possessed. He had been offered forty pounds for it; but a good collie was worth more than that, more than anything, to a "herd"; he did the herd's work for him. "As for the like of them!" he would cry, and scornfully indicate the scouring tails of his assistants.

Once—I translate John's Lallan, for I cannot do it justice, being born *Britannis in montibus*, indeed, but alas! *inerudito sæculo*—once, in the days of his good dog, he had bought some sheep in Edinburgh, and on the way out, the road being crowded, two were lost. This was a reproach to John, and a slur upon the dog; and both were alive to their misfortune. Word came, after some days, that a farmer about Braid had found a pair of sheep; and thither went John and the dog to ask for restitution. But the farmer was a hard man and stood upon his rights. "How were they marked?" he asked; and since John had bought right and left from many sellers and had no notion of the marks—"Very well," said the farmer, "then it's only right that I should keep them."—"Well," said John, "it's a fact that I cannae tell the sheep; but if my dog can, will ye let me have them?" The farmer was honest as well as hard, and besides I daresay he had little fear of the ordeal; so he had all the sheep upon his farm into one large park, and turned John's dog into their midst. That hairy man of business knew his errand well; he knew that John and he had bought two sheep and (to their shame) lost them about Boroughmuirhead; he knew besides (the Lord knows how, unless by listening) that they were come to Braid for their recovery; and without pause or blunder singled out, first one and then another, the two waifs. It was that afternoon the forty pounds were offered and refused. And the shepherd and his dog—what do I say? the true shepherd and his man—set off together by Fairmilehead in jocund humour, and "smiled to ither" all the way home, with the two recovered ones before them. So far, so good; but intelligence may be abused. The dog, as he is by little man's inferior in mind, is only by little his superior in virtue; and John had another collie tale of quite a different complexion. At the foot of the moss behind Kirk Yetton (Caer Ketton, wise men say) there is a scrog of low wood and a pool with a dam for washing sheep. John was one day lying under a bush in the scrog, when he was aware of a collie on the far hillside skulking down through the deepest of the heather with obtrusive stealth. He knew the dog; knew him for a clever, rising practitioner from quite a distant farm; one whom perhaps he had coveted as he saw him masterfully steering flocks to market. But what did the practitioner so far from home? and why this guilty and secret manœuvring towards the pool?—for it was towards the pool that he was heading. John lay the closer under his bush, and presently saw the dog come forth upon the margin, look all about him to see if he were anywhere observed, plunge in and repeatedly wash himself over head and ears, and then (but now openly and with tail in air) strike homeward over the hills. That same night word was sent his master, and the rising practitioner, shaken up from where he lay, all innocence, before the fire, was had out to a dykeside and promptly shot; for alas! he was that foulest of criminals under trust, a sheep-eater; and it was from the maculation of sheep's blood that he had come so far to cleanse himself in the pool behind Kirk Yetton.

A trade that touches nature, one that lies at the foundations of life, in which we have all had ancestors employed, so that on a hint of it ancestral memories revive, lends itself to literary use, vocal or written. The fortune of a tale lies not alone in the skill of him that writes, but as much, perhaps, in the inherited experience of him who reads; and when I hear with a particular thrill of things that I have never done or seen, it is one of that innumerable army of my ancestors rejoicing in past deeds. Thus novels begin to touch not the fine *dilettanti* but the gross mass of mankind, when they leave off to speak of parlours and shades of manner and still-born niceties of motive, and begin to deal with fighting, sailoring, adventure, death or childbirth; and thus ancient outdoor crafts and occupations, whether Mr. Hardy wields the shepherd's crook or Count Tolstoi swings the scythe, lift romance into a near neighbourhood with epic. These aged things have on them the dew of man's morning; they lie near, not so much to us, the semi-artificial flowerets, as to the trunk and aboriginal taproot of the race. A thousand interests spring up in the process of the ages, and a thousand perish; that is now an eccentricity or a lost art which was once the fashion of an empire; and those only are perennial matters that rouse us to-day, and that roused men in all epochs of the past. There is a certain critic, not indeed of execution but of matter, whom I dare be known to set before the best: a certain low-browed, hairy gentleman, at first a percher in the fork of trees, next (as they relate) a dweller in caves, and whom I think I see squatting in cave-mouths, of a pleasant afternoon, to munch his berries—his wife, that accomplished lady, squatting by his side: his name I never heard, but he is often described as Probably Arboreal, which may serve for recognition. Each has his own tree of ancestors, but at the top of all sits Probably Arboreal; in all our veins there run some minims of his old, wild, tree-top blood; our civilised nerves still tingle with his rude terrors and pleasures; and to that which would have moved our common ancestor, all must obediently thrill.

We have not so far to climb to come to shepherds; and it may be I had one for an ascendant who has largely moulded me. But yet I think I owe my taste for that hillside business rather to the art and interest of John Todd. He it was that made it live for me, as the artist can make all things live. It was through him the simple strategy of massing sheep upon a snowy evening, with its attendant scampering of earnest, shaggy aides-de-camp, was an affair that I never wearied of seeing, and that I never weary of recalling to mind: the shadow of the night darkening on the hills, inscrutable black blots of snow shower moving here and there like night already come, huddles of yellow sheep and dartings of black dogs upon the snow, a bitter air that took you by the throat, unearthly harpings of the wind along the moors; and for centre-piece to all these features and influences, John winding up the brae, keeping his captain's eye upon all sides, and breaking, ever and again, into a spasm of bellowing that seemed to make the evening bleaker. It is thus that I still see him in my mind's eye, perched on a hump of the declivity not far from Halkerside, his staff in airy flourish, his great voice taking hold upon the hills and echoing terror to the lowlands; I, meanwhile, standing somewhat back, until the fit should be over, and, with a pinch of snuff, my friend relapse into his easy, even conversation.

VII

The Manse

I HAVE named, among many rivers that make music in my memory, that dirty Water of Leith. Often and often I desire to look upon it again; and the choice of a point of view is easy to me. It should be at a certain water-door, embowered in shrubbery. The river is there dammed back for the service of the flour-mill just below, so that it lies deep and darkling, and the sand slopes into brown obscurity with a glint of gold; and it has but newly been recruited by the borrowings of the snuff-mill just above, and these, tumbling merrily in, shake the pool to its black heart, fill it with drowsy eddies, and set the curded froth of many other mills solemnly steering to and fro upon the surface. Or so it was when I was young; for change, and the masons, and the pruning-knife, have been busy; and if I could hope to repeat a cherished experience, it must be on many and impossible conditions. I must choose, as well as the point of view, a certain moment in my growth, so that the scale may be exaggerated, and the trees on the steep opposite side may seem to climb to heaven, and the sand by the water-door, where I am standing, seem as low as Styx. And I must choose the season also, so that the valley may be brimmed like a cup with sunshine and the songs of birds;—and the year of grace, so that when I turn to leave the riverside I may find the old manse and its inhabitants unchanged.

It was a place in that time like no other: the garden cut into provinces by a great hedge of beech, and overlooked by the church and the terrace of the churchyard, where the tombstones were thick, and after nightfall "spunkies" might be seen to dance at least by children; flower-plots lying warm in sunshine; laurels and the great yew making elsewhere a pleasing horror of shade; the smell of water rising from all round, with an added tang of paper-mills; the sound of water everywhere, and the sound of mills—the wheel and the dam singing their alternate strain; the birds on every bush and from every corner of the overhanging woods pealing out their notes until the air throbbed with them; and in the midst of this, the manse. I see it, by the standard of my childish stature, as a great and roomy house. In truth, it was not so large as I supposed, nor yet so convenient, and, standing where it did, it is difficult to suppose that it was healthful. Yet a large family of stalwart sons and tall daughters were housed and reared, and came to man and womanhood in that nest of little chambers; so that the face of the earth was peppered with the children of the manse, and letters with outlandish stamps became familiar to the local postman, and the walls of the little chambers brightened with the wonders of the East. The dullest could see this was a house that had a pair of hands in divers foreign places: a well-beloved house—its image fondly dwelt on by many travellers.

Here lived an ancestor of mine, who was a herd of men. I read him, judging with older criticism the report of childish observation, as a man of singular simplicity of nature; unemotional, and hating the display of what he felt; standing contented on the old ways; a lover of his life and innocent habits to the end. We children admired him: partly for his beautiful face and silver hair, for none more than children are concerned for beauty and, above all, for beauty in the old; partly for the solemn light in which we beheld him once a week, the observed of all observers, in the pulpit. But his strictness and distance, the effect, I now fancy, of old age, slow blood, and settled habit, oppressed us with a kind of terror. When not abroad, he sat much alone, writing sermons or letters to his scattered family in a dark and cold room with a library of bloodless books—or so they seemed in those days, although I have some of them now on my own shelves and like well enough to read them; and these lonely hours wrapped him in the greater gloom for our imaginations. But the study had a redeeming grace in many Indian pictures, gaudily coloured and dear to young eyes. I cannot depict (for I have no such passions now) the greed with which I beheld them ; and when I was once sent in to say a psalm to my grandfather, I went, quaking indeed with fear, but at the same time glowing with hope that, if I said it well, he might reward me with an Indian picture.

> "Thy foot He'll not let slide, nor will
> He slumber that thee keeps,"

it ran : a strange conglomerate of the unpronounceable, a sad model to set in childhood before one who was himself to be a versifier, and a task in recitation that really merited reward. And I must suppose the old man thought so too, and was either touched or amused by the performance ; for he took me in his arms with most unwonted tenderness, and kissed me, and gave me a little kindly sermon for my psalm ; so that, for that day, we were clerk and parson. I was struck by this reception into so tender a surprise that I forgot my disappointment. And indeed the hope was one of those that childhood forges for a pastime, and with no design upon reality. Nothing was more unlikely than that my grandfather should strip himself of one of those pictures, love-gifts and reminders of his absent sons ; nothing more unlikely than that he should bestow it upon me. He had no idea of spoiling children, leaving all that to my aunt ; he had fared hard himself, and blubbered under the rod in the last century ; and his ways were still

Spartan for the young. The last word I heard upon his lips was in this Spartan key. He had overwalked in the teeth of an east wind, and was now near the end of his many days. He sat by the dining-room fire, with his white hair, pale face and bloodshot eyes, a somewhat awful figure; and my aunt had given him a dose of our good old Scotch medicine, Dr. Gregory's powder. Now that remedy, as the work of a near kinsman of Rob Roy himself, may have a savour of romance for the imagination; but it comes uncouthly to the palate. The old gentleman had taken it with a wry face; and that being accomplished, sat with perfect simplicity, like a child's, munching a "barley-sugar kiss." But when my aunt, having the canister open in her hands, proposed to let me share in the sweets, he interfered at once. I had had no Gregory; then I should have no barley-sugar kiss: so he decided with a touch of irritation. And just then the phaeton coming opportunely to the kitchen door—for such was our unlordly fashion—I was taken for the last time from the presence of my grandfather.

Now I often wonder what I have inherited from this old minister. I must suppose, indeed, that he was fond of preaching sermons, and so am I, though I never heard it maintained that either of us loved to hear them. He sought health in his youth in the Isle of Wight, and I have sought it in both hemispheres; but whereas he found and kept it, I am still on the quest. He was a great lover of Shakespeare, whom he read aloud, I have been told, with taste; well, I love my Shakespeare also, and am persuaded I can read him well, though I own I never have been told so. He made embroidery, designing his own patterns; and in that kind of work I never made anything but a kettle-holder in Berlin wool, and an odd garter of knitting, which was as black as the chimney before I had done with it. He loved port, and nuts, and porter; and so do I, but they agreed better with my grandfather, which seems to me a breach of contract. He had chalk-stones in his fingers; and these, in good time, I may possibly inherit, but I would much rather have inherited his noble presence. Try as I please, I cannot join myself on with the reverend doctor; and all the while, no doubt, and even as I write the phrase, he moves in my blood, and whispers words to me, and sits efficient in the very knot and centre of my being. In his garden, as I played there, I learned the love of mills—or had I an ancestor a miller?—and a kindness for the neighbourhood of graves, as homely things not without their poetry—or had I an ancestor a sexton? But what of the garden where he played himself?—for that, too, was a scene of my education. Some part of me played there in the eighteenth century, and ran races under the green avenue at Pilrig; some part of me trudged up Leith Walk, which was still a country place, and sat on the High School benches, and was thrashed, perhaps, by Dr. Adam. The house where I spent my youth was not yet thought upon; but we made holiday parties among the cornfields on its site, and ate strawberries and cream near by at a gardener's. All this I had forgotten; only my grandfather remembered and once reminded me. I have forgotten, too, how we grew up, and took orders, and went to our first Ayrshire parish, and fell in love with and married a daughter of Burns's Dr. Smith—"Smith opens out his cauld harangues." I have forgotten, but I was there all the same, and heard stories of Burns at first hand.

And there is a thing stranger than all that; for this *homunculus* or part-man of mine that walked about the eighteenth century with Dr. Balfour in his youth, was in the way of meeting other *homunculos* or part-men, in the persons of my other ancestors. These were of a lower order and doubtless we looked down upon them duly. But as I went to college with Dr. Balfour, I may have seen the lamp and oil man taking down the shutters from his shop beside the Tron;—we may have had a rabbit-hutch or a bookshelf made for us by a certain carpenter in I know not what wynd of the old, smoky city; or, upon some holiday excursion, we may have looked into the windows of a cottage in a flower-garden and seen a certain weaver plying his shuttle. And these were all kinsmen of mine upon the other side; and from the eyes of the lamp and oil man one-half of my unborn father, and one-quarter of myself, looked out upon us as we went by to college. Nothing of all this would cross the mind of the young student, as he posted up the Bridges with trim, stockinged legs, in that city of cocked hats and good Scotch still unadulterated. It would not cross his mind that he should have a daughter; and the lamp and oil man, just then beginning, by a not unnatural metastasis, to bloom into a lighthouse-engineer, should have a grandson; and that these two, in the fulness of time, should wed; and some portion of that student himself should survive yet a year or two longer in the person of their child.

But our ancestral adventures are beyond even the arithmetic of fancy; and it is the chief recommendation of long pedigrees, that we can follow backward the careers of our *homunculos* and be reminded of our antenatal lives. Our conscious years are but a moment in the history of the elements that build us. Are you a bank-clerk, and do you live at Peckham? It was not always so. And though to-day I am only a man of letters, either tradition errs or I was present when there landed at St. Andrews a French barber-surgeon, to tend the health and the beard of the great Cardinal Beaton; I have shaken a spear in the Debateable Land and shouted the slogan of the Elliots; I was present when a skipper, plying from Dundee, smuggled Jacobites to France after the '15; I was in a West India merchant's office, perhaps next door to Bailie Nicol Jarvie's, and managed the business of a plantation in St. Kitt's; I was with my engineer-grandfather (the son-in-law of the lamp and oil man) when he sailed north about Scotland on the famous cruise that gave us the *Pirate* and the *Lord of the Isles;* I was with him, too, on the Bell Rock, in the fog, when the *Smeaton* had drifted from her moorings, and the Aberdeen men, pick in hand, had seized upon the only boats, and he must stoop and lap sea-water before his tongue could utter audible words; and once more with him when the Bell Rock beacon took a "thrawe," and his workmen fled into the tower, then nearly finished, and he sat unmoved reading in his Bible—or affecting to read—till one after another slunk back with confusion of countenance to their engineer. Yes, parts of me have seen life, and met adventures, and sometimes met them well. And away in the still cloudier past, the threads that make me up can be traced by fancy into the bosoms of thousands and millions of ascendants: Picts who rallied round Macbeth and the old (and highly preferable) system of descent by females, fleërs from before the legions of Agricola, marchers in Pannonian morasses, star-gazers on Chaldæan plateaus; and, furthest of all, what face is this that fancy can see peering through the disparted branches? What sleeper in green tree-tops, what muncher of nuts, concludes my pedigree? Probably arboreal in his habits. . . .

And I know not which is the more strange, that I should carry about with me some fibres of my minister-grandfather; or that in him, as he sat in his cool study, grave, reverend, contented gentleman, there was an aboriginal frisking of the blood that was not his; tree-top memories, like undeveloped negatives, lay dormant in his mind; tree-top instincts awoke and were trod down; and Probably Arboreal (scarce to be distinguished from a monkey) gambolled and chattered in the brain of the old divine.

VIII

Memoirs of an Islet

THOSE who try to be artists use, time after time, the matter of their recollections, setting and resetting little coloured memories of men and scenes, rigging up (it may be) some especial friend in the attire of a buccaneer, and decreeing armies to manœuvre, or murder to be done, on the playground of their youth. But the memories are a fairy gift which cannot be worn out in using. After a dozen services in various tales, the little sunbright pictures of the past still shine in the mind's eye with not a lineament defaced, not a tint impaired. *Glück und Unglück wird Gesang*, if Goethe pleases; yet only by endless avatars, the original re-embodying after each. So that a writer, in time, begins to wonder at the perdurable life of these impressions; begins, perhaps, to fancy that he wrongs them when he weaves them in with fiction; and looking back on them with ever-growing kindness, puts them at last, substantive jewels, in a setting of their own.

One or two of these pleasant spectres I think I have laid. I used one but the other day: a little eyot of dense, freshwater sand, where I once waded deep in butterburrs, delighting to hear the song of the river on both sides, and to tell myself that I was indeed and at last upon an island. Two of my puppets lay there a summer's day, hearkening to the shearers at work in riverside fields and to the drums of the gray old garrison upon the neighbouring hill. And this was, I think, done rightly: the place was rightly peopled—and now belongs not to me but to my puppets—for a time at least. In time, perhaps, the puppets will grow faint; the original memory swim up instant as ever; and I shall once more lie in bed, and see the little sandy isle in Allan Water as it is in nature, and the child (that once was me) wading there in butterburrs; and wonder at the instancy and virgin freshness of that memory; and be pricked again, in season and out of season, by the desire to weave it into art.

There is another isle in my collection, the memory of which besieges me. I put a whole family there, in one of my tales; and later on, threw upon its shores, and condemned to several days of rain and shellfish on its tumbled boulders, the hero of another. The ink is not yet faded; the sound of the sentences is still in my mind's ear; and I am under a spell to write of that island again.

I

The little isle of Earraid lies close in to the south-west corner of the Ross of Mull: the sound of Iona on one side, across which you may see the isle and church of Columba; the open sea to the other, where you shall be able to mark, on a clear, surfy day, the breakers running white on many sunken rocks. I first saw it, or first remembered seeing it, framed in the round bull's-eye of a cabin port, the sea lying smooth along its shores like the waters of a lake, the colourless, clear light of the early morning making plain its heathery and rocky hummocks. There stood upon it, in these days, a single rude house of uncemented stones, approached by a pier of wreckwood. It must have been very early, for it was then summer, and in summer, in that latitude, day scarcely withdraws; but even at that hour the house was making a sweet smoke of peats which came to me over the bay, and the bare-legged daughters of the cotter were wading by the pier. The same day we visited the shores of the isle in the ship's boats; rowed deep into Fiddler's Hole, sounding as we went; and having taken stock of all possible accommodation, pitched on the northern inlet as the scene of operations. For it was no accident that had brought the lighthouse steamer to anchor in the Bay of Earraid. Fifteen miles away to seaward, a certain black rock stood environed by the

Atlantic rollers, the outpost of the Torran reefs. Here was a tower to be built, and a star lighted, for the conduct of seamen. But as the rock was small, and hard of access, and far from land, the work would be one of years; and my father was now looking for a shore station, where the stones might be quarried and dressed, the men live, and the tender, with some degree of safety, lie at anchor.

I saw Earraid next from the stern thwart of an Iona lugger, Sam Bough and I sitting there cheek by jowl, with our feet upon our baggage, in a beautiful, clear, northern summer eve. And behold! there was now a pier of stone, there were rows of sheds, railways, travelling-cranes, a street of cottages, an iron house for the resident engineer, wooden bothies for the men, a stage where the courses of the tower were put together experimentally, and behind the settlement a great gash in the hillside where granite was quarried. In the bay, the steamer lay at her moorings. All day long there hung about the place the music of chinking tools; and even in the dead of night, the watchman carried his lantern to and fro in the dark settlement, and could light the pipe of any midnight muser. It was, above all, strange to see Earraid on the Sunday, when the sound of the tools ceased and there fell a crystal quiet. All about the green compound men would be sauntering in their Sunday's best, walking with those lax joints of the reposing toiler, thoughtfully smoking, talking small, as if in honour of the stillness, or hearkening to the wailing of the gulls. And it was strange to see our Sabbath services, held, as they were, in one of the bothies, with Mr. Brebner reading at a table, and the congregation perched about in the double tier of sleeping bunks; and to hear the singing of the psalms, "the chapters," the inevitable Spurgeon's sermon, and the old, eloquent lighthouse prayer.

In fine weather, when by the spy-glass on the hill the sea was observed to run low upon the reef, there would be a sound of preparation in the very early morning; and before the sun had risen from behind Ben More, the tender would steam out of the bay. Over fifteen sea-miles of the great blue Atlantic rollers she ploughed her way, trailing at her tail a brace of wallowing stone-lighters. The open ocean widened upon either board, and the hills of the mainland began to go down on the horizon, before she came to her unhomely destination, and lay-to at last where the rock clapped its black head above the swell, with the tall iron barrack on its spider legs, and the truncated tower, and the cranes waving their arms, and the smoke of the engine-fire rising in the mid-sea. An ugly reef is this of the Dhu-Heartach; no pleasant assemblage of shelves, and pools, and creeks, about which a child might play for a whole summer without weariness, like the Bell Rock or the Skerryvore, but one oval nodule of black-trap, sparsely bedabbled with an inconspicuous fucus, and alive in every crevice with a dingy insect between a slater and a bug. No other life was there but that of sea-birds, and of the sea itself, that here ran like a mill-race, and growled about the outer reef for ever, and ever and again, in the calmest weather, roared and spouted on the rock itself. Times were different upon Dhu-Heartach when it blew, and the night fell dark, and the neighbour lights of Skerryvore and Rhu-val were quenched in fog, and the men sat prisoned high up in their iron drum, that then resounded with the lashing of the sprays. Fear sat with them in their sea-beleaguered dwelling; and the colour changed in anxious faces when some greater billow struck the barrack, and its pillars quivered and sprang under the blow. It was then that the foreman builder, Mr. Goodwillie, whom I see before me still in his rock-habit of undecipherable rags, would get his fiddle down and strike up human minstrelsy amid the music of the storm. But it was in sunshine only that I saw Dhu-Heartach; and it was in sunshine, or the yet lovelier summer afterglow, that the steamer would return to Earraid, ploughing an enchanted sea; the obedient lighters, relieved of their deck cargo, riding in her wake more quietly; and the steersman upon each, as she rose on the long swell, standing tall and dark against the shining west.

II

But it was in Earraid itself that I delighted chiefly. The lighthouse settlement scarce encroached beyond its fences; over the top of the first brae the ground was all virgin, the world all shut out, the face of things unchanged by any of man's doings. Here was no living presence, save for the limpets on the rocks, for some old, gray, rain-beaten ram that I might rouse out of a ferny den betwixt two boulders, or for the haunting and the piping of the gulls. It was older than man; it was found so by incoming Celts, and seafaring Norsemen, and Columba's priests. The earthy savour of the bog-plants, the rude disorder of the boulders, the inimitable seaside brightness of the air, the brine and the iodine, the lap of the billows among the weedy reefs, the sudden springing up of a great run of dashing surf along the sea-front of the isle, all that I saw and felt my predecessors must have seen and felt with scarce a difference. I steeped myself in open air and in past ages.

"Delightful would it be to me to be in *Uchd Ailiun*
  On the pinnacle of a rock,
That I might often see
  The face of the ocean;
That I might hear the song of the wonderful birds,
  Source of happiness;

That I might hear the thunder of the crowding waves
Upon the rocks:
At times at work without compulsion—
This would be delightful;
At times plucking dulse from the rocks;
At times at fishing."

So, about the next island of Iona, sang Columba himself twelve hundred years before. And so might I have sung of Earraid.

And all the while I was aware that this life of sea-bathing and sun-burning was for me but a holiday. In that year cannon were roaring for days together on French battlefields; and I would sit in my isle (I call it mine, after the use of lovers) and think upon the war, and the loudness of these far-away battles, and the pain of the men's wounds, and the weariness of their marching. And I would think too of that other war which is as old as mankind, and is indeed the life of man: the unsparing war, the grinding slavery of competition; the toil of seventy years, dear-bought bread, precarious honour, the perils and pitfalls, and the poor rewards. It was a long look forward; the future summoned me as with trumpet calls, it warned me back as with a voice of weeping and beseeching; and I thrilled and trembled on the brink of life, like a childish bather on the beach.

There was another young man on Earraid in these days, and we were much together, bathing, clambering on the boulders, trying to sail a boat and spinning round instead in the oily whirlpools of the roost. But the most part of the time we spoke of the great uncharted desert of our futures; wondering together what should there befall us; hearing with surprise the sound of our own voices in the empty vestibule of youth. As far, and as hard, as it seemed then to look forward to the grave, so far it seems now to look backward upon these emotions; so hard to recall justly that loath submission, as of the sacrificial bull, with which we stooped our necks under the yoke of destiny. I met my old companion but the other day; I cannot tell of course what he was thinking; but, upon my part, I was wondering to see us both so much at home, and so composed and sedentary in the world; and how much we had gained, and how much we had lost, to attain to that composure; and which had been upon the whole our best estate: when we sat there prating sensibly like men of some experience, or when we shared our timorous and hopeful counsels in a western islet.

IX

Thomas Stevenson, Civil Engineer

THE death of Thomas Stevenson will mean not very much to the general reader. His service to mankind took on forms of which the public knows little and understands less. He came seldom to London, and then only as a task, remaining always a stranger and a convinced provincial; putting up for years at the same hotel where his father had gone before him; faithful for long to the same restaurant, the same church, and the same theatre, chosen simply for propinquity; steadfastly refusing to dine out. He had a circle of his own, indeed, at home; few men were more beloved in Edinburgh, where he breathed an air that pleased him; and wherever he went, in railway carriages or hotel smoking-rooms, his strange, humorous vein of talk, and his transparent honesty, raised him up friends and admirers. But to the general public and the world of London, except about the parliamentary committee-rooms, he remained unknown. All the time, his lights were in every part of the world, guiding the mariner; his firm were consulting engineers to the Indian, the New

Zealand, and the Japanese Lighthouse Boards, so that Edinburgh was a world centre for that branch of applied science; in Germany, he had been called "the Nestor of lighthouse illumination"; even in France, where his claims were long denied, he was at last, on the occasion of the late Exposition, recognised and medalled. And to show by one instance the inverted nature of his reputation, comparatively small at home, yet filling the world, a friend of mine was this winter on a visit to the Spanish main, and was asked by a Peruvian if he "knew Mr. Stevenson the author, because his works were much esteemed in Peru?" My friend supposed the reference was to the writer of tales; but the Peruvian had never heard of *Dr. Jekyll;* what he had in his eye, what was esteemed in Peru, were the volumes of the engineer.

Thomas Stevenson was born at Edinburgh in the year 1818, the grandson of Thomas Smith, first engineer to the Board of Northern Lights, son of Robert Stevenson, brother of Alan and David; so that his nephew, David Alan Stevenson, joined with him at the time of his death in the engineership, is the sixth of the family who has held, successively or conjointly, that office. The Bell Rock, his father's great triumph, was finished before he was born; but he served under his brother Alan in the building of Skerryvore, the noblest of all extant deep-sea lights; and, in conjunction with his brother David, he added two—the Chickens and Dhu-Heartach—to that small number of man's extreme outposts in the ocean. Of shore lights, the two brothers last named erected no fewer than twenty-seven; of beacons,* about twenty-five. Many harbours were successfully carried out: one, the harbour of Wick, the chief disaster of my father's life, was a failure; the sea proved too strong for man's arts; and after expedients hitherto unthought of, and on a scale hyper-cyclopean, the work must be deserted, and now stands a ruin in that bleak, God-forsaken bay, ten miles from John-o'-Groat's. In the improvement of rivers the brothers were likewise in a large way of practice over both England and Scotland, nor had any British engineer anything approaching their experience.

It was about this nucleus of his professional labours that all my father's scientific inquiries and inventions centred; these proceeded from, and acted back upon, his daily business. Thus it was as a harbour engineer that he became interested in the propagation and reduction of waves; a difficult subject in regard to which he has left behind him much suggestive matter and some valuable approximate results. Storms were his sworn adversaries, and it was through the study of storms that he approached that of meteorology at large. Many who knew him not otherwise, knew—perhaps have in their gardens—his louvre-

* In Dr. Murray's admirable new dictionary, I have remarked a flaw *sub voce* Beacon. In its express, technical sense, a beacon may be defined as "a founded, artificial sea-mark, not lighted."

boarded screen for instruments. But the great achievement of his life was, of course, in optics as applied to lighthouse illumination. Fresnel had done much; Fresnel had settled the fixed light apparatus on a principle that still seems unimprovable; and when Thomas Stevenson stepped in and brought to a comparable perfection the revolving light, a not unnatural jealousy and much painful controversy rose in France. It had its hour; and, as I have told already, even in France it has blown by. Had it not, it would have mattered the less, since all through his life my father continued to justify his claim by fresh advances. New apparatus for lights in new situations was continually being designed with the same unwearied search after perfection, the same nice ingenuity of means; and though the holophotal revolving light perhaps still remains his most elegant contrivance, it is difficult to give it the palm over the much later condensing system, with its thousand possible modifications. The number and the value of these improvements entitle their author to the name of one of mankind's benefactors. In all parts of the world a safer landfall awaits the mariner. Two things must be said: and, first, that Thomas Stevenson was no mathematician. Natural shrewdness, a sentiment of optical laws, and a great intensity of consideration led him to just conclusions; but to calculate the necessary formulæ for the instruments he had conceived was often beyond him, and he must fall back on the help of others, notably on that of his cousin and lifelong intimate friend, *emeritus* Professor Swan, of St. Andrews, and his later friend, Professor P. G. Tait. It is a curious enough circumstance, and a great encouragement to others, that a man so ill-equipped should have succeeded in one of the most abstract and arduous walks of applied science. The second remark is one that applies to the whole family, and only particularly to Thomas Stevenson from the great number and importance of his inventions: holding as the Stevensons did a Government appointment, they regarded their original work as something due already to the nation, and none of them has ever taken out a patent. It is another cause of the comparative obscurity of the name: for a patent not only brings in money, it infallibly spreads reputation; and my father's instruments enter anonymously into a hundred light-rooms, and are passed anonymously over in a hundred reports, where the least considerable patent would stand out and tell its author's story.

But the life-work of Thomas Stevenson remains; what we have lost, what we now rather try to recall, is the friend and companion. He was a man of a somewhat antique strain: with a blended sternness and softness that was wholly Scottish and at first somewhat bewildering; with a profound essential melancholy of disposition and (what often accompanies it) the most humorous geniality in company; shrewd and childish; passionately attached, passionately prejudiced; a man of many extremes, many faults of temper, and no very stable foothold for himself among life's troubles. Yet he was a wise adviser; many men, and these not inconsiderable, took counsel with him habitually. "I sat at his feet," writes one of these, "when I asked his advice, and when the broad brow was set in thought and the firm mouth said his say, I always knew that no man could add to the worth of the conclusion." He had excellent taste, though whimsical and partial; collected old furniture and delighted specially in sunflowers long before the days of Mr. Wilde; took a lasting pleasure in prints and pictures; was a devout admirer of Thomson of Duddingston at a time when few shared the taste; and though he read little, was constant to his favourite books. He had never any Greek; Latin he happily re-taught himself after he had left school, where he was a mere consistent idler: happily, I say, for Lactantius, Vossius, and Cardinal Bona were his chief authors. The first he must have read for twenty years uninterruptedly, keeping it near him in his study, and carrying it in his bag on journeys. Another old theologian, Brown of Wamphray, was often in his hands. When he was indisposed, he had two books, *Guy Mannering* and *The Parent's Assistant*, of which he never wearied. He was a strong Conservative, or, as he preferred to call himself, a Tory; except in so far as his views were modified by a hot-headed chivalrous sentiment for women. He was actually in favour of a marriage law under which any woman might have a divorce for the asking, and no man on any ground whatever; and the same sentiment found another expression in a Magdalen Mission in Edinburgh, founded and largely supported by himself. This was but one of the many channels of his public generosity; his private was equally unstrained. The Church of Scotland, of which he held the doctrines (though in a sense of his own) and to which he bore a clansman's loyalty, profited often by his time and money; and though, from a morbid sense of his own unworthiness, he would never consent to be an office-bearer, his advice was often sought, and he served the Church on many committees. What he perhaps valued highest in his work were his contributions to the defence of Christianity; one of which, in particular, was praised by Hutchinson Stirling and reprinted at the request of Professor Crawford.

His sense of his own unworthiness I have called morbid; morbid, too, were his sense of the fleetingness of life and his concern for death. He had never accepted the conditions of man's life or his own character; and his inmost thoughts were ever tinged with the Celtic melancholy. Cases of conscience were sometimes grievous to him, and that delicate employment of a scientific witness cost him many qualms. But he found respite from these troublesome humours in his work, in his lifelong study of natural science, in the society of those he loved, and in his daily walks, which now would carry him far into the country with some congenial friend, and now keep him dangling about the town from one old book-shop to another, and scraping romantic acquaintance with every dog that passed. His talk, compounded of so much sterling sense and so much freakish humour, and clothed in language so apt, droll, and emphatic, was a perpetual delight to all who knew him before the clouds began to settle on his mind. His use of language was both just and picturesque ; and when at the beginning of his illness he began to feel the ebbing of this power, it was strange and painful to hear him reject one word after another as inadequate, and at length desist from the search and leave his phrase unfinished rather than finish it without propriety. It was perhaps another Celtic trait that his affections and emotions, passionate as these were, and liable to passionate ups and downs, found the most eloquent expression both in words and gestures. Love, anger, and indignation shone through him and broke forth in imagery, like what we read of Southern races. For all these emotional extremes, and in spite of the melancholy ground of his character, he had upon the whole a happy life ; nor was he less fortunate in his death, which at the last came to him unaware.

X

Talk and Talkers

Sir, we had a good talk.—Johnson.

As we must account for every idle word, so we must for every idle silence.—Franklin.

I

THERE can be no fairer ambition than to excel in talk; to be affable, gay, ready, clear and welcome; to have a fact, a thought, or an illustration, pat to every subject; and not only to cheer the flight of time among our intimates, but bear our part in that great international congress, always sitting, where public wrongs are first declared, public errors first corrected, and the course of public opinion shaped, day by day, a little nearer to the right. No measure comes before Parliament but it has been long ago prepared by the grand jury of the talkers; no book is written that has not been largely composed by their assistance. Literature in many of its branches is no other than the shadow of good talk; but the imitation falls far short of the original in life, freedom and effect. There are always two to a talk, giving and taking, comparing experience and according conclusions. Talk is fluid, tentative, continually "in further search and progress"; while written words remain fixed, become idols even to the writer, found wooden dogmatisms, and preserve flies of obvious error in the amber of the truth. Last and chief, while literature, gagged with linsey-woolsey, can only deal with a fraction of the life of man, talk goes fancy-free and may call a spade a spade. Talk has none of the freezing immunities of the pulpit. It cannot, even if it would, become merely æsthetic or merely classical like literature. A jest intervenes, the solemn humbug is dissolved in laughter, and speech runs forth out of the contemporary groove into the open fields of nature, cheery and cheering, like schoolboys out of school. And it is in talk alone that we can learn our period and ourselves. In short, the first duty of a man is to speak; that is his chief business in this world; and talk, which is the harmonious speech of two or more, is by far the most accessible of pleasures. It costs nothing in money; it is all profit; it completes our education, founds and fosters our friendships, and can be enjoyed at any age and in almost any state of health.

The spice of life is battle; the friendliest relations are still a kind of contest; and if we would not forego all that is valuable in our lot, we must continually face some other person, eye to eye, and wrestle a fall whether in love or enmity. It is still by force of body, or power of character or intellect, that we attain to worthy pleasures. Men and women contend for each other in the lists of love, like rival mesmerists; the active and adroit decide their challenges in the sports of the body; and the sedentary sit down to chess or conversation. All sluggish and pacific pleasures are, to the same degree, solitary and selfish; and every durable bond between human beings is founded in or heightened by some element of competition. Now, the relation that has the least root in matter is undoubtedly that airy one of friendship; and hence, I suppose, it is that good talk most commonly arises among friends. Talk is, indeed, both the scene and instrument of friendship. It is in talk alone that the friends can measure strength and enjoy that amicable counter-assertion of personality which is the gauge of relations and the sport of life.

A good talk is not to be had for the asking. Humours must first be accorded in a kind of overture or prologue; hour, company and circumstance be suited; and then, at a fit juncture, the subject, the quarry of two heated minds, spring up like a deer out of the wood. Not that the talker has any of the hunter's pride, though he has all and more than all his ardour. The genuine artist follows the stream of conversation as an angler follows the windings of a brook, not dallying where he fails to "kill." He trusts implicitly to hazard; and he is rewarded by continual variety, continual pleasure, and those changing prospects of the truth that are the best of education. There is nothing in a subject, so called, that we should regard it as an idol, or follow it beyond the promptings of desire. Indeed, there are few subjects; and so far as they are truly talkable, more than the half of them may be reduced to three: that I am I, that you are you, and that there are other people dimly understood to be not quite the same as either. Wherever talk may range, it still runs half the time on these eternal lines. The theme being set, each plays on himself as on an instrument; asserts and justifies himself; ransacks his brain for instances and opinions, and brings them forth new-minted, to his own surprise and the admiration of his adversary. All natural talk is a festival of ostentation; and by the laws of the game each accepts and fans the vanity of the other. It is from that reason that we venture to lay ourselves so open, that we dare to be so warmly eloquent, and that we swell in each other's eyes to such a vast proportion. For talkers, once launched, begin to overflow the limits of their ordinary selves, tower up to the height of their secret pretensions, and give themselves out for the heroes, brave, pious, musical and wise, that in their most shining moments they aspire to be. So they weave for themselves with words and for a while inhabit a palace of delights, temple at once and theatre, where they fill the round of the world's dignities, and feast with the gods, exulting in Kudos. And when the talk is over, each goes his way, still flushed with vanity and admiration, still trailing clouds of glory; each declines from the height of his ideal orgie, not in a moment, but by slow declension. I remember, in the *entr'acte* of an afternoon performance, coming forth into the sunshine, in a beautiful green, gardened corner of a romantic city; and as I sat and smoked, the music moving in my blood, I seemed to sit there and evaporate *The Flying Dutchman* (for it was that I had been hearing) with a wonderful sense of life, warmth, well-being and pride; and the noises of the city, voices, bells and marching feet, fell together in my ears like a symphonious orchestra. In the same way, the excitement of a good talk lives for a long while after in the blood, the heart still hot within you, the brain still simmering, and the physical earth swimming around you with the colours of the sunset.

Natural talk, like ploughing, should turn up a large surface of life, rather than dig mines into geological strata. Masses of experience, anecdote, incident, cross-lights, quotation, historical instances, the whole flotsam and jetsam of two minds forced in and in upon the matter in hand from every point of the compass, and from every degree of mental elevation and abasement—these are the material with which talk is fortified, the food on which the talkers thrive. Such argument as is proper to the exercise should still be brief and seizing. Talk should proceed by instances; by the apposite, not the expository. It should keep close along the lines of humanity, near the bosoms and businesses of men, at the level where history, fiction and experience intersect and illuminate each other. I am I, and You are You, with all my heart; but conceive how these lean propositions change and brighten when, instead of words, the actual you and I sit cheek by jowl, the spirit housed in the live body, and the very clothes uttering voices to corroborate the story in the face. Not less surprising is the change when we leave off to speak of generalities—the bad, the good, the miser, and all the characters of Theophrastus—and call up other men, by anecdote or instance, in their very trick and feature; or trading on a common knowledge, toss each other famous names, still glowing with the hues of life. Communication is no longer by words, but by the instancing of whole biographies, epics, systems of philosophy, and epochs of history, in bulk. That which is understood excels that which is spoken in quantity and quality alike; ideas thus figured and personified, change hands, as we may say, like coin; and the speakers imply without effort the most obscure and intricate thoughts. Strangers who have a large common ground of reading will, for this reason, come the sooner to the grapple of genuine converse. If they know Othello and Napoleon, Consuelo and Clarissa Harlowe, Vautrin and Steenie Steenson, they can leave generalities and begin at once to speak by figures.

Conduct and art are the two subjects that arise most frequently and that embrace the widest range of facts. A few pleasures bear discussion for their own sake, but only those which are most social or most radically human; and even these can only be discussed among their devotees. A technicality is always welcome to the expert, whether in athletics, art or law; I have heard the best kind of talk on technicalities from such rare and happy persons as both know and love their business. No human being ever spoke of scenery for above two minutes at a time, which makes me suspect we hear too much of it in literature. The weather is regarded as the very nadir and scoff of conversational topics. And yet the weather, the dramatic element in scenery, is far more tractable in language, and far more human both in import and suggestion than the stable features of the landscape. Sailors and shepherds, and the people generally of coast and mountain, talk well of it; and it is often excitingly presented in literature. But the tendency of all living talk draws it back and back into the common focus of humanity. Talk is a creature of the street and market-place, feeding on gossip; and its last resort is still in a discussion on morals. That is the heroic form of gossip; heroic in virtue of its high pretensions; but still gossip, because it turns on personalities. You can keep no men long, nor Scotchmen at all, off moral or theological discussion. These are to all the world what law is to lawyers; they are everybody's technicalities; the medium through which all consider life, and the dialect in which they express their judgments. I knew three young men who walked together daily for some two months in a solemn and beautiful forest and in cloudless summer weather; daily they talked with unabated zest, and yet scarce wandered that whole time beyond two subjects—theology and love. And perhaps neither a court of love nor an assembly of divines would have granted their premisses or welcomed their conclusions.

Conclusions, indeed, are not often reached by talk any more than by private thinking. That is not the profit. The profit is in the exercise, and above all in the experience; for when we reason at large on any subject, we review our state and history in life. From time to time, however, and specially, I think, in talking art, talk becomes effective, conquering like war, widening the boundaries of knowledge like an exploration. A point arises; the question takes a problematical, a baffling, yet a likely air; the talkers begin to feel lively presentiments of some conclusion near at hand; towards this they strive with emulous ardour, each by his own path, and struggling for first utterance; and then one leaps upon the summit of that matter with a shout, and almost at the same moment the other is beside him; and behold they are agreed. Like enough, the progress is illusory, a mere cat's cradle having been wound and unwound out of words. But the sense of joint discovery is none the less giddy and inspiriting. And in the life of the talker such triumphs, though imaginary, are neither few nor far apart; they are attained with speed and pleasure, in the hour of mirth; and by the nature of the process, they are always worthily shared.

There is a certain attitude, combative at once and deferential, eager to fight yet most averse to quarrel, which marks out at once the talkable man. It is not eloquence, not fairness, not obstinacy, but a certain proportion of all of these that I love to encounter in my amicable adversaries. They must not be pontiffs holding doctrine, but huntsmen questing after elements of truth. Neither must they be boys to be instructed, but fellow-teachers with whom I may wrangle and agree on equal terms. We must reach some solution, some shadow of consent; for without that, eager talk becomes a torture. But we do not wish to reach it cheaply, or quickly, or without the tussle and effort wherein pleasure lies.

The very best talker, with me, is one whom I shall call Spring-Heel'd Jack. I say so, because I never knew any one who mingled so largely the possible ingredients of converse. In the Spanish proverb, the fourth man necessary to compound a salad, is a madman to mix it: Jack is that madman. I know not which is more remarkable; the insane lucidity of his conclusions, the humorous eloquence of his language, or his power of method, bringing the whole of life into the focus of the subject treated, mixing the conversational salad like a drunken god. He doubles like the serpent, changes and flashes like the shaken kaleidoscope, transmigrates bodily into the views of others, and so, in the twinkling of an eye and with a heady rapture, turns questions inside out and flings them empty before you on the ground, like a triumphant conjuror. It is my common practice when a piece of conduct puzzles me, to attack it in the presence of Jack with such grossness, such partiality and such wearing iteration, as at length shall spur him up in its defence. In a moment he transmigrates, dons the required character, and with moonstruck philosophy justifies the act in question. I can fancy nothing to compare with the *vim* of these impersonations, the strange scale of language, flying from Shakespeare to Kant, and from Kant to Major Dyngwell—

> "As fast as a musician scatters sounds
> Out of an instrument——"

the sudden, sweeping generalisations, the absurd irrelevant particularities, the wit, wisdom, folly, humour, eloquence and bathos, each startling in its kind, and yet all luminous in the admired disorder of their combination. A talker of a different calibre, though belonging to the same school, is Burly. Burly is a man of a great presence; he commands a larger atmosphere, gives the impression of a grosser mass of character than most men. It has been said of him that his presence could be felt in a room you entered blindfold; and the same, I think, has been said of other powerful constitutions condemned to much physical inaction. There is something boisterous and piratic in Burly's manner of talk which suits well enough with this impression. He will roar you down, he will bury his face in his hands, he will undergo passions of revolt and agony; and meanwhile his attitude of mind is really both conciliatory and receptive; and after Pistol has been out-Pistol'd, and the welkin rung for hours, you begin to perceive a certain subsidence in these spring torrents, points of agreement issue, and you end arm-in-arm, and in a glow of mutual admiration. The outcry only serves to make your final union the more unexpected and precious. Throughout there has been perfect sincerity, perfect intelligence, a desire to hear although not always to listen, and an unaffected eagerness to meet concessions. You have, with Burly, none of the dangers that attend debate with Spring-Heel'd Jack; who may at any moment turn his powers of transmigration on yourself, create for you a view you never held, and then furiously fall on you for holding it. These, at least, are my two favourites, and both are loud, copious, intolerant talkers. This argues that I myself am in the same category; for if we love talking at all, we love a bright, fierce adversary, who will hold his ground, foot by foot, in much our own manner, sell his attention dearly, and give us our full measure of the dust and exertion of battle. Both these men can be beat from a position, but it takes six hours to do it; a high and hard adventure, worth attempting. With both you can pass days in an enchanted country of the mind, with people, scenery and manners of its own; live a life apart, more arduous, active and glowing than any real existence; and come forth again when the talk is over, as out of a theatre or a dream, to find the east wind still blowing and the chimney-pots of the old battered city still around you. Jack has the far finer mind, Burly the far more honest; Jack gives us the animated poetry, Burly the romantic prose, of similar themes; the one glances high like a meteor and makes a light in darkness; the other, with many changing hues of fire, burns at the sea-level, like a conflagration; but both have the same humour and artistic interests, the same unquenched ardour in pursuit, the same gusts of talk and thunderclaps of contradiction.

Cockshot * is a different article, but vastly entertaining, and has been meat and drink to me for many a long evening. His manner is dry, brisk and pertinacious, and the choice of words not much. The point about him is his extraordinary readiness and spirit. You can propound nothing but he has either a theory about it

* The late Fleeming Jenkin.

ready-made, or will have one instantly on the stocks, and proceed to lay its timbers and launch it in your presence. "Let me see," he will say. "Give me a moment. I *should* have some theory for that." A blither spectacle than the vigour with which he sets about the task, it were hard to fancy. He is possessed by a demoniac energy, welding the elements for his life, and bending ideas, as an athlete bends a horseshoe, with a visible and lively effort. He has, in theorising, a compass, an art; what I would call the synthetic gusto; something of a Herbert Spencer, who should see the fun of the thing. You are not bound, and no more is he, to place your faith in these brand-new opinions. But some of them are right enough, durable even for life; and the poorest serve for a cock-shy—as when idle people, after picnics, float a bottle on a pond and have an hour's diversion ere it sinks. Whichever they are, serious opinions or humours of the moment, he still defends his ventures with indefatigable wit and spirit, hitting savagely himself, but taking punishment like a man. He knows and never forgets that people talk, first of all, for the sake of talking; conducts himself in the ring, to use the old slang, like a thorough "glutton," and honestly enjoys a telling facer from his adversary. Cockshot is bottled effervescency, the sworn foe of sleep. Three-in-the-morning Cockshot, says a victim. His talk is like the driest of all imaginable dry champagnes. Sleight of hand and inimitable quickness are the qualities by which he lives. Athelred, on the other hand, presents you with the spectacle of a sincere and somewhat slow nature thinking aloud. He is the most unready man I ever knew to shine in conversation. You may see him sometimes wrestle with a refractory jest for a minute or two together, and perhaps fail to throw it in the end. And there is something singularly engaging, often instructive, in the simplicity with which he thus exposes the process as well as the result, the works as well as the dial of the clock. Withal he has his hours of inspiration. Apt words come to him as if by accident, and, coming from deeper down, they smack the more personally, they have the more of fine old crusted humanity, rich in sediment and humour. There are sayings of his in which he has stamped himself into the very grain of the language; you would think he must have worn the words next his skin and slept with them. Yet it is not as a sayer of particular good things that Athelred is most to be regarded, rather as the stalwart woodman of thought. I have pulled on a light cord often enough, while he has been wielding the broad-axe; and between us, on this unequal division, many a specious fallacy has fallen. I have known him to battle the same question night after night for years, keeping it in the reign of talk, constantly applying it and re-applying it to life with humorous or grave intention, and all the while, never hurrying, nor flagging, nor taking an unfair advantage of the facts. Jack at a given moment, when arising, as it were, from the tripod, can be more radiantly just to those from whom he differs; but then the tenor of his thoughts is even calumnious; while Athelred, slower to forge excuses, is yet slower to condemn, and sits over the welter of the world, vacillating but still judicial, and still faithfully contending with his doubts.

Both the last talkers deal much in points of conduct and religion studied in the "dry light" of prose. Indirectly and as if against his will the same elements from time to time appear in the troubled and poetic talk of Opalstein. His various and exotic knowledge, complete although unready sympathies, and fine, full, discriminative flow of language, fit him out to be the best of talkers; so perhaps he is with some, not *quite* with me—*proxime accessit*, I should say. He sings the praises of the earth and the arts, flowers and jewels, wine and music, in a moonlight, serenading manner, as to the light guitar; even wisdom comes from his tongue like singing; no one is, indeed, more tuneful in the upper notes. But even while he sings the song of the Sirens, he still hearkens to the barking of the Sphinx. Jarring Byronic notes interrupt the flow of his Horatian humours. His mirth has something of the tragedy of the world for its perpetual background; and he feasts like Don Giovanni to a double orchestra, one lightly sounding for the dance, one pealing Beethoven in the distance. He is not truly reconciled either with life or with himself; and this instant war in his members sometimes divides the man's attention. He does not always, perhaps not often, frankly surrender himself in conversation. He brings into the talk other thoughts than those which he expresses; you are conscious that he keeps an eye on something else, that he does not shake off the world, nor quite forget himself. Hence arise occasional disappointments; even an occasional unfairness for his companions, who find themselves one day giving too much, and the next, when they are wary out of season, giving perhaps too little. Purcel is in another class from any I have mentioned. He is no debater, but appears in conversation, as occasion rises, in two distinct characters, one of which I admire and fear, and the other love. In the first, he is radiantly civil and rather silent, sits on a high, courtly hilltop, and from that vantage-ground drops you his remarks like favours. He seems not to share in our sublunary contentions; he wears no sign of interest; when on a sudden there falls in a crystal of wit, so polished that the dull do not perceive it, but so right that the sensitive are silenced. True talk should have more body and blood, should be louder, vainer and more declaratory of the man; the true talker should not hold so steady an advantage over whom he speaks with; and that is one reason out of a score why I prefer my Purcel in his second character, when he unbends into a strain of graceful gossip, singing like the fireside kettle. In these moods he has an elegant homeliness that rings of the true Queen Anne. I know another person who attains, in his moments, to the insolence of a Restoration comedy, speaking, I declare, as Congreve wrote; but that is a sport of nature, and scarce falls under the rubric, for there is none, alas! to give him answer.

One last remark occurs: It is the mark of genuine conversation that the sayings can scarce be quoted with their full effect beyond the circle of common friends. To have their proper weight they should appear in a biography, and with the portrait of the speaker. Good talk is dramatic; it is like an impromptu piece of acting where each should represent himself to the greatest advantage; and that is the best kind of talk where each speaker is most fully and candidly himself, and where, if you were to shift the speeches round from one to another, there would be the greatest loss in significance and perspicuity. It is for this reason that talk depends so wholly on our company. We should like to introduce Falstaff and Mercutio, or Falstaff and Sir Toby; but Falstaff in talk with Cordelia seems even painful. Most of us, by the Protean quality of man, can talk to some degree with all; but the true talk, that strikes out all the slumbering best of us, comes only with the peculiar brethren of our spirits, is founded as deep as love in the constitution of our being, and is a thing to relish with all our energy, while yet we have it, and to be grateful for forever.

XI

Talk and Talkers *

II

IN the last paper there was perhaps too much about mere debate; and there was nothing said at all about that kind of talk which is merely luminous and restful, a higher power of silence, the quiet of the evening shared by ruminating friends. There is something, aside from personal preference, to be alleged in support of this omission. Those who are no chimney-cornerers who rejoice in the social thunderstorm, have a ground in reason for their choice. They get little rest indeed; but restfulness is a quality for cattle; the virtues are all active, life is alert, and it is in repose that men prepare themselves for evil. On the other hand, they are bruised into a knowledge of themselves and others; they have in a high degree the fencer's pleasure in dexterity displayed and proved; what they get they get upon life's terms, paying for it as they go; and once the talk is launched, they

* This sequel was called forth by an excellent article in *The Spectator*.

are assured of honest dealing from an adversary eager like themselves. The aboriginal man within us, the cave-dweller, still lusty as when he fought tooth and nail for roots and berries, scents this kind of equal battle from afar; it is like his old primæval days upon the crags, a return to the sincerity of savage life from the comfortable fictions of the civilised. And if it be delightful to the Old Man, it is none the less profitable to his younger brother, the conscientious gentleman. I feel never quite sure of your urbane and smiling coteries; I fear they indulge a man's vanities in silence, suffer him to encroach, encourage him on to be an ass, and send him forth again, not merely contemned for the moment, but radically more contemptible than when he entered. But if I have a flushed, blustering fellow for my opposite, bent on carrying a point, my vanity is sure to have its ears rubbed, once at least, in the course of the debate. He will not spare me when we differ; he will not fear to demonstrate my folly to my face.

For many natures there is not much charm in the still, chambered society, the circle of bland countenances, the digestive silence, the admired remark, the flutter of affectionate approval. They demand more atmosphere and exercise; "a gale upon their spirits," as our pious ancestors would phrase it; to have their wits well breathed in an uproarious Valhalla. And I suspect that the choice, given their character and faults, is one to be defended. The purely wise are silenced by facts; they talk in a clear atmosphere, problems lying around them like a view in nature; if they can be shown to be somewhat in the wrong, they digest the reproof like a thrashing, and make better intellectual blood. They stand corrected by a whisper; a word or a glance reminds them of the great eternal law. But it is not so with all. Others in conversation seek rather contact with their fellow-men than increase of knowledge or clarity of thought. The drama, not the philosophy, of life is the sphere of their intellectual activity. Even when they pursue truth, they desire as much as possible of what we may call human scenery along the road they follow. They dwell in the heart of life; the blood sounding in their ears, their eyes laying hold of what delights them with a brutal avidity that makes them blind to all besides, their interest riveted on people, living, loving, talking, tangible people. To a man of this description, the sphere of argument seems very pale and ghostly. By a strong expression, a perturbed countenance, floods of tears, an insult which his conscience obliges him to swallow, he is brought round to knowledge which no syllogism would have conveyed to him. His own experience is so vivid, he is so superlatively conscious of himself, that if, day after day, he is allowed to hector and hear nothing but approving echoes, he will lose his hold on the soberness of things and take himself in earnest for a god. Talk might be to such an one the very way of moral ruin; the school where he might learn to be at once intolerable and ridiculous.

This character is perhaps commoner than philosophers suppose. And for persons of that stamp to learn much by conversation, they must speak with their superiors, not in intellect, for that is a superiority that must be proved, but in station. If they cannot find a friend to bully them for their good, they must find either an old man, a woman, or some one so far below them in the artificial order of society, that courtesy may be particularly exercised.

The best teachers are the aged. To the old our mouths are always partly closed; we must swallow our obvious retorts and listen. They sit above our heads, on life's raised daïs, and appeal at once to our respect and pity. A flavour of the old school, a touch of something different in their manner—which is freer and rounder, if they come of what is called a good family, and often more timid and precise if they are of the middle class—serves, in these days, to accentuate the difference of age and add a distinction to gray hairs. But their superiority is founded more deeply than by outward marks or gestures. They are before us in the march of man; they have more or less solved the irking problem; they have battled through the equinox of life; in good and evil they have held their course; and now, without open shame, they near the crown and harbour. It may be we have been struck with one of fortune's darts; we can scarce be civil, so cruelly is our spirit tossed. Yet long before we were so much as thought upon, the like calamity befell the old man or woman that now, with pleasant humour, rallies us upon our inattention, sitting composed in the holy evening of man's life, in the clear shining after rain. We grow ashamed of our distresses, new and hot and coarse, like villainous roadside brandy; we see life in aerial perspective, under the heavens of faith; and out of the worst, in the mere presence of contented elders, look forward and take patience. Fear shrinks before them "like a thing reproved," not the flitting and ineffectual fear of death, but the instant, dwelling terror of the responsibilities and revenges of life. Their speech, indeed, is timid; they report lions in the path; they counsel a meticulous footing; but their serene, marred faces are more eloquent and tell another story. Where they have gone, we will go also, not very greatly fearing; what they have endured unbroken, we also, God helping us, will make a shift to bear.

Not only is the presence of the aged in itself remedial, but their minds are stored with antidotes, wisdom's simples, plain considerations overlooked by youth. They have matter to communicate, be they never so stupid. Their talk is not merely literature, it is great literature; classic in virtue of the speaker's detachment, studded, like a book of travel, with things we should not otherwise have learnt. In virtue, I have said, of the speaker's detachment,—and this is why, of two old men, the one who is not your father speaks to you with the more sensible authority; for in the paternal relation the oldest have lively interests and remain still young. Thus I have known two young men great friends; each swore by the other's father; the father of each swore by the other lad; and yet each pair of parent and child were perpetually by the ears. This is typical: it reads like the germ of some kindly comedy.

The old appear in conversation in two characters: the critically silent and the garrulous anecdotic. The last is perhaps what we look for; it is perhaps the more instructive. An old gentleman, well on in years, sits handsomely and naturally in the bow-window of his age, scanning experience with reverted eye; and chirping and smiling, communicates the accidents and reads the lesson of his long career. Opinions are strengthened, indeed, but they are also weeded out in the course of years. What remains steadily present to the eye of the retired veteran in his hermitage, what still ministers to his content, what still quickens his old honest heart—these are "the real long-lived things" that Whitman tells us to prefer. Where youth agrees with age, not where they differ, wisdom lies; and it is when the young disciple finds his heart to beat in tune with his gray-bearded teacher's that a lesson may be learned. I have known one old gentleman, whom I may name, for he is now gathered to his stock—Robert Hunter, Sheriff of Dumbarton, and author of an excellent law-book still re-edited and republished. Whether he was originally big or little is more than I can guess. When I knew him he was all fallen away and fallen in; crooked and shrunken; buckled into a stiff waistcoat for support; troubled by ailments, which kept him hobbling in and out of the room; one foot gouty; a wig for decency, not for deception, on his head; close shaved, except under his chin—and for that he never failed to apologise, for it went sore against the traditions of his life. You can imagine how he would fare in a novel by Miss Mather; yet this rag of a Chelsea veteran lived to his last year in the plenitude of all that is best in man, brimming with human kindness, and staunch as a Roman soldier under his manifold infirmities. You could not say that he had lost his memory, for he would repeat Shakespeare and Webster and Jeremy Taylor and Burke by the page together; but the parchment was filled up, there was no room for fresh inscriptions, and he was capable of repeating the same anecdote on many successive visits. His voice survived in its full power, and he took a pride in using it. On his last voyage as Commissioner of Lighthouses, he hailed a ship at sea and made himself clearly audible without a speaking trumpet, ruffling the while with a proper vanity in his achievement. He had a habit of eking out his words with interrogative hems, which was puzzling and a little wearisome, suited ill with his appearance, and seemed a survival from some former stage of bodily portliness. Of yore, when he was a great pedestrian and no enemy to good claret, he may have pointed with these minute-guns his allocutions to the bench. His humour was perfectly equable, set beyond the reach of fate; gout, rheumatism, stone and gravel might have combined their forces against that frail tabernacle, but when I came round on Sunday evening, he would lay aside Jeremy Taylor's *Life of Christ* and greet me with the same open brow, the same kind formality of manner. His opinions and sympathies dated the man almost to a decade. He had begun life, under his mother's influence, as an admirer of Junius, but on maturer knowledge had transferred his admiration to Burke. He cautioned me, with entire gravity, to be punctilious in writing English; never to forget that I was a Scotchman, that English was a foreign tongue, and that if I attempted the colloquial, I should certainly be shamed: the remark was apposite, I suppose, in the days of David Hume. Scott was too new for him; he had known the author—known him, too, for a Tory; and to the genuine classic a contemporary is always something of a trouble. He had the old, serious love of the play; had even, as he was proud to tell, played a certain part in the history of Shakespearian revivals, for he had successfully pressed on Murray, of the old Edinburgh Theatre, the idea of producing Shakespeare's fairy pieces with great scenic display. A moderate in religion, he was much struck in the last years of his life by a conversation with two young lads, revivalists "H'm," he would say—"new to me. I have had—h'm—no such experience." It struck him, not with pain, rather with a solemn philosophic interest, that he, a Christian as he hoped, and a Christian of so old a standing, should hear these young fellows talking of his own subject, his own weapons that he had fought the battle of life with,—"and—h'm—not understand." In this wise and graceful attitude he did justice to himself and others, reposed unshaken in his old beliefs, and recognised their limits without anger or alarm. His last recorded remark, on the last night of his life, was after he had been arguing against Calvinism with his minister and was interrupted by an intolerable pang. "After all," he said, "of all the 'isms, I know none so bad as rheumatism." My own last sight of him was some time before, when we dined together at an inn; he had been on circuit, for he stuck to his duties like a chief part of his existence; and I remember it as the only occasion on which he ever soiled his lips with slang—a thing he loathed. We were both Roberts; and as we took our places at table, he addressed me with a twinkle: "We are just what you would call two bob." He offered me port, I remember, as the proper milk of youth; spoke of "twenty-shilling notes"; and throughout the meal was full of old-world pleasantry and quaintness, like an ancient boy on a holiday. But what I recall chiefly was his confession that he had never read *Othello* to an end. Shakespeare was his continual study. He loved nothing better than to display his knowledge and memory by adducing parallel passages from Shakespeare, passages where the same word was employed, or the same idea differently treated. But *Othello* had beaten him. "That noble gentleman and that noble lady—h'm—too painful for me." The same night the hoardings were covered with posters, "Burlesque of *Othello*," and the contrast blazed up in my mind like a bonfire. An unforgettable look it gave me into that kind man's soul. His acquaintance was indeed a liberal and pious education. All the humanities were taught in that bare dining-room beside his gouty footstool. He was a piece of good advice; he was himself the instance that pointed and adorned his various talk. Nor could a young man have found elsewhere a place so set apart from envy, fear, discontent, or any of the passions that debase; a life so honest and composed; a soul like an ancient violin, so subdued to harmony, responding to a touch in music—as in that dining-room, with Mr. Hunter chatting at the eleventh hour, under the shadow of eternity, fearless and gentle.

The second class of old people are not anecdotic; they are rather hearers than talkers, listening to the young with an amused and critical attention. To have this sort of intercourse to perfection, I think we must go to old ladies. Women are better hearers than men, to begin with; they learn, I fear in anguish, to bear with the tedious and infantile vanity of the other sex; and we will take more from a woman than even from the oldest man in the way of biting comment. Biting comment is the chief part, whether for profit or amusement, in this business. The old lady that I have in my eye is a very caustic speaker, her tongue, after years of practice, in absolute command, whether for silence or attack. If she chance to dislike you, you will be tempted to curse the malignity of age. But if you chance to please even slightly, you will be listened to with a particular laughing grace of sympathy, and from time to time chastised, as if in play, with a parasol as heavy as a pole-axe. It requires a singular art, as well as the vantage-ground of age, to deal these stunning corrections among the coxcombs of the young. The pill is disguised in sugar of wit; it is administered as a compliment—if you had not pleased, you would not have been censured; it is a personal affair—a hyphen, a *trait d'union*, between you and your censor; age's philandering, for her pleasure and your good. Incontestably the young man feels very much of a fool; but he must be a perfect Malvolio, sick with self-love, if he cannot take an open buffet and still smile. The correction of silence is what kills; when you know you have transgressed, and your friend says nothing and avoids your eye. If a man were made of gutta-percha, his heart would quail at such a moment. But when the word is out, the worst is over; and a fellow with any good-humour at all may pass through a perfect hail of witty criticism, every bare place on his soul hit to the quick with a shrewd missile, and reappear, as if after a dive, tingling with a fine moral reaction, and ready, with a shrinking readiness, one-third loath, for a repetition of the discipline.

There are few women, not well sunned and ripened, and perhaps toughened, who can thus stand apart from a man and say the true thing with a kind of genial cruelty. Still there are some—and I doubt if there be any man who can return the compliment. The class of man represented by Vernon Whitford in *The Egoist* says, indeed, the true thing, but he says it stockishly. Vernon is a noble fellow, and makes, by the way, a noble and instructive contrast to Daniel Deronda; his conduct is the conduct of a man of honour; but we agree with him, against our consciences, when he remorsefully considers "its astonishing dryness." He is the best of men, but the best of women manage to combine all that and something more. Their very faults assist them; they are helped even by the falseness of their position in life. They can retire into the fortified camp of the proprieties. They can touch a subject and suppress it. The most adroit employ a somewhat elaborate reserve as a means to be frank, much as they wear gloves when they shake hands. But a man has the full responsibility of his freedom, cannot evade a question, can scarce be silent without rudeness, must answer for his words upon the moment, and is not seldom left face to face with a damning choice, between the more or less dishonourable wriggling of Deronda and the downright woodenness of Vernon Whitford.

But the superiority of women is perpetually menaced; they do not sit throned on infirmities like the old; they are suitors as well as sovereigns; their vanity is engaged, their affections are too apt to follow; and hence much of the talk between the sexes degenerates into something unworthy of the name. The desire to please, to shine with a certain softness of lustre and to draw a fascinating picture of oneself, banishes from conversation all that is sterling and most of what is humorous. As soon as a strong current of mutual admiration begins to flow, the human interest triumphs entirely over the intellectual, and the commerce of words, consciously or not, becomes secondary to the commercing of eyes. But even where this ridiculous danger is avoided, and a man and woman converse equally and honestly, something in their nature or their education falsifies the strain. An instinct prompts them to agree; and where that is impossible, to agree to differ. Should they neglect the warning, at the first suspicion of an argument, they find themselves in different hemispheres. About any point of business or conduct, any actual affair demanding settlement, a woman will speak and listen, hear and answer arguments, not only with natural wisdom, but with candour and logical honesty. But if the subject of debate be something in the air, an abstraction, an excuse for talk, a logical Aunt Sally, then may the male debater instantly abandon hope; he may employ reason, adduce facts, be supple, be smiling, be angry, all shall avail him nothing; what the woman said first, that (unless she has forgotten it) she will repeat at the end. Hence, at the very junctures when a talk between men grows brighter and quicker, and begins to promise to bear fruit, talk between the sexes is menaced with dissolution. The point of difference, the point of interest, is evaded by the brilliant woman, under a shower of irrelevant conversational rockets; it is bridged by the discreet woman with a rustle of silk, as she passes smoothly forward to the nearest point of safety. And this sort of prestidigitation, juggling the dangerous topic out of sight until it can be reintroduced with safety in an altered shape, is a piece of tactics among the true drawing-room queens.

The drawing-room is, indeed, an artificial place; it is so by our choice and for our sins. The subjection of women; the ideal imposed upon them from the cradle, and worn, like a hair-shirt, with so much constancy; their motherly, superior tenderness to man's vanity and self-importance; their managing arts—the arts of a civilised slave among good-natured barbarians—are all painful ingredients and all help to falsify relations. It is not till we get clear of that amusing artificial scene that genuine relations are founded, or ideas honestly compared. In the garden, on the road or the hillside, or *tête-à-tête* and apart from interruptions, occasions arise when we may learn much from any single woman; and nowhere more often than in married life. Marriage is one long conversation, chequered by disputes. The disputes are valueless; they but ingrain the difference; the heroic heart of woman prompting her at once to nail her colours to the mast. But in the intervals, almost unconsciously and with no desire to shine, the whole material of life is turned over and over, ideas are struck out and shared, the two persons more and more adapt their notions one to suit the other, and in process of time, without sound of trumpet, they conduct each other into new worlds of thought.

XII

The Character of Dogs

THE civilisation, the manners, and the morals of dog-kind are to a great extent subordinated to those of his ancestral master, man. This animal, in many ways so superior, has accepted a position of inferiority, shares the domestic life, and humours the caprices of the tyrant. But the potentate, like the British in India, pays small regard to the character of his willing client, judges him with listless glances, and condemns him in a byword. Listless have been the looks of his admirers, who have exhausted idle terms of praise, and buried the poor soul below exaggerations. And yet more idle, and, if possible, more unintelligent has been the attitude of his express detractors; those who are very fond of dogs "but in their proper place"; who say "poo' fellow, poo' fellow," and are themselves far poorer; who whet the knife of the vivisectionist or heat his oven; who are not ashamed to admire "the creature's instinct"; and flying far beyond folly, have dared to resuscitate the theory of animal machines. The "dog's instinct" and the "automaton-dog," in this age of psychology and science, sound like strange anachronisms. An automaton he certainly is; a machine working independently of his control, the heart, like the mill-wheel, keeping all in motion, and the consciousness, like a person shut in the mill garret, enjoying the view out of the window and shaken by the thunder of the stones; an automaton in one corner of which a living spirit is confined: an automaton like man. Instinct again he certainly possesses. Inherited aptitudes are his, inherited frailties. Some things he at once views and understands, as though he were awakened from a sleep, as though he came "trailing clouds of glory." But with him, as with man, the field of instinct is limited; its utterances are obscure and occasional; and about the far larger part of life both the dog and his master must conduct their steps by deduction and observation.

The leading distinction between dog and man, after and perhaps before the different duration of their lives, is that the one can speak and that the other cannot. The absence of the power of speech confines the dog in the development of his intellect. It hinders him from many speculations, for words are the beginning of metaphysic. At the same blow it saves him from many superstitions, and his silence has won for him a higher name for virtue than his conduct justifies. The faults of the dog are many. He is vainer than man, singularly greedy of notice, singularly intolerant of ridicule, suspicious like the deaf, jealous to the degree of frenzy, and radically devoid of truth. The day of an intelligent small dog is passed in the manufacture and the laborious communication of falsehood; he lies with his tail, he lies with his eye, he lies with his protesting paw; and when he rattles his dish or scratches at the door his purpose is other than appears. But he has some apology to offer for the vice. Many of the signs which form his dialect have come to bear an arbitrary meaning, clearly understood both by his master and himself; yet when a new want arises he must either invent a new vehicle of meaning or wrest an old one to a different purpose; and this necessity frequently recurring must tend to lessen his idea of the sanctity of symbols. Meanwhile the dog is clear in his own conscience, and draws, with a human nicety, the distinction between formal and essential truth. Of his punning perversions, his legitimate dexterity with symbols, he is even vain; but when he has told and been detected in a lie, there is not a hair upon his body but confesses guilt. To a dog of gentlemanly feeling theft and falsehood are disgraceful vices. The canine, like the human, gentleman demands in his misdemeanours Montaigne's "*je ne sais quoi de généreux.*" He is never more than half ashamed of having barked or bitten; and for those faults into which he has been led by the desire to shine before a lady of his race, he retains, even under physical correction, a share of pride. But to be caught lying, if he understands it, instantly uncurls his fleece.

Just as among dull observers he preserves a name for truth, the dog has been credited with modesty. It is amazing how the use of language blunts the faculties of man—that because vain-glory finds no vent in words, creatures supplied with eyes have been unable to detect a fault so gross and obvious. If a small spoiled dog were suddenly to be endowed with speech, he would prate interminably, and still about himself; when we had friends, we should be forced to lock him in a garret; and what with his whining jealousies and his foible for falsehood, in a year's time he would have gone far to weary out our love. I was about to compare him to Sir Willoughby Patterne, but the Patternes have a manlier sense of their own merits; and the parallel, besides, is ready. Hans Christian Andersen, as we behold him in his startling memoirs, thrilling from top to toe with an excruciating vanity, and scouting even along the street for shadows of offence—here was the talking dog.

It is just this rage for consideration that has betrayed the dog into his satellite position as the friend of man. The cat, an animal of franker appetites, preserves his independence. But the dog, with one eye ever on the audience, has been wheedled into slavery, and praised and patted into the renunciation of his nature. Once he ceased hunting and became man's plate-licker, the Rubicon was crossed. Thenceforth he was a gentleman of leisure; and except the few whom we keep working, the whole race grew more and more self-conscious, mannered and affected. The number of things that a small dog does naturally is strangely small. Enjoying better spirits and not crushed under material cares, he is far more theatrical than average man. His whole life, if he be a dog of any pretension to gallantry, is spent in a vain show, and in the hot pursuit of admiration. Take out your puppy for a walk, and you will find the little ball of fur clumsy, stupid, bewildered, but natural. Let but a few months pass, and when you repeat the process you will find nature buried in convention. He will do nothing plainly; but the simplest processes of our material life will all be bent into the forms of an elaborate and mysterious etiquette. Instinct, says the fool, has awakened. But it is not so. Some dogs—some, at the very least—if they be kept separate from others, remain quite natural; and these, when at length they meet with a companion of experience, and have the game explained to them, distinguish themselves by the severity of their devotion to its rules. I wish I were allowed to tell a story which would radiantly illuminate the point; but men, like dogs, have an elaborate and mysterious etiquette. It is their bond of sympathy that both are the children of convention.

The person, man or dog, who has a conscience is eternally condemned to some degree of humbug; the sense of the law in their members fatally precipitates either towards a frozen and affected bearing. And the converse is true;

and in the elaborate and conscious manners of the dog, moral opinions and the love of the ideal stand confessed. To follow for ten minutes in the street some swaggering, canine cavalier, is to receive a lesson in dramatic art and the cultured conduct of the body; in every act and gesture you see him true to a refined conception; and the dullest cur, beholding him, pricks up his ear and proceeds to imitate and parody that charming ease. For to be a high-mannered and high-minded gentleman, careless, affable, and gay, is the inborn pretension of the dog. The large dog, so much lazier, so much more weighed upon with matter, so majestic in repose, so beautiful in effort, is born with the dramatic means to wholly represent the part. And it is more pathetic and perhaps more instructive to consider the small dog in his conscientious and imperfect efforts to outdo Sir Philip Sidney. For the ideal of the dog is feudal and religious; the ever-present polytheism, the whip-bearing Olympus of mankind, rules them on the one hand; on the other, their singular difference of size and strength among themselves effectually prevents the appearance of the democratic notion. Or we might more exactly compare their society to the curious spectacle presented by a school—ushers, monitors, and big and little boys—qualified by one circumstance, the introduction of the other sex. In each, we should observe a somewhat similar tension of manner, and somewhat similar points of honour. In each the larger animal keeps a contemptuous good-humour; in each the smaller annoys him with wasp-like impudence, certain of practical immunity; in each we shall find a double life producing double characters, and an excursive and noisy heroism combined with a fair amount of practical timidity. I have known dogs, and I have known school heroes that, set aside the fur, could hardly have been told apart; and if we desire to understand the chivalry of old, we must turn to the school playfields or the dungheap where the dogs are trooping.

Woman, with the dog, has been long enfranchised. Incessant massacre of female innocents has changed the proportions of the sexes and perverted their relations. Thus, when we regard the manners of the dog, we see a romantic and monogamous animal, once perhaps as delicate as the cat, at war with impossible conditions. Man has much to answer for; and the part he plays is yet more damnable and parlous than Corin's in the eyes of Touchstone. But his intervention has at least created an imperial situation for the rare surviving ladies. In that society they reign without a rival: conscious queens; and in the only instance of a canine wife-beater that has ever fallen under my notice, the criminal was somewhat excused by the circumstances of his story. He is a little, very alert, well-bred, intelligent Skye, as black as a hat, with a wet bramble for a nose and two cairngorms for eyes. To the human observer, he is decidedly well-looking; but to the ladies of his race he seems abhorrent. A thorough elaborate gentleman, of the plume and sword-knot order, he was born with a nice sense of gallantry to women. He took at their hands the most outrageous treatment; I have heard him bleating like a sheep, I have seen him streaming blood, and his ear tattered like a regimental banner; and yet he would scorn to make reprisals. Nay more, when a human lady upraised the contumelious whip against the very dame who had been so cruelly misusing him, my little great-heart gave but one hoarse cry and fell upon the tyrant tooth and nail. This is the tale of a soul's tragedy. After three years of unavailing chivalry, he suddenly, in one hour, threw off the yoke of obligation; had he been Shakespeare he would then have written *Troilus and Cressida* to brand the offending sex; but being only a little dog, he began to bite them. The surprise of the ladies whom he attacked indicated the monstrosity of his offence; but he had fairly beaten off his better angel, fairly committed moral suicide; for almost in the same hour, throwing aside the last rags of decency, he proceeded to attack the aged also. The fact is worth remark, showing, as it does, that ethical laws are common both to dogs and men; and that with both a single deliberate violation of the conscience loosens all. "But while the lamp holds on to burn," says the paraphrase, "the greatest sinner may return." I have been cheered to see symptoms of effectual penitence in my sweet ruffian; and by the handling that he accepted uncomplainingly the other day from an indignant fair one, I begin to hope the period of *Sturm und Drang* is closed.

All these little gentlemen are subtle casuists. The duty to the female dog is plain; but where competing duties rise, down they will sit and study them out, like Jesuit confessors. I knew another little Skye, somewhat plain in manner and appearance, but a creature compact of amiability and solid wisdom. His family going abroad for a winter, he was received for that period by an uncle in the same city. The winter over, his own family home again, and his own house (of which he was very proud) reopened, he found himself in a dilemma between two conflicting duties of loyalty and gratitude. His old friends were not to be neglected, but it seemed hardly decent to desert the new. This was how he solved the problem. Every morning, as soon as the door was opened, off posted Coolin to his uncle's, visited the children in the nursery, saluted the whole family, and was back at home in time for breakfast and his bit of fish. Nor was this done without a sacrifice on his part, sharply felt; for he had to forego the particular honour and jewel of his day—his morning's walk with my father. And, perhaps from this cause, he gradually wearied of and relaxed the practice, and at length returned entirely to his ancient habits. But the same decision served him in another and more distressing case of divided duty, which happened not long after. He was not at all a kitchen dog, but the cook had nursed him with unusual kindness during the distemper; and though he did not adore her as he adored my father—although (born snob) he was critically conscious of her position as "only a servant"—he still cherished for her a special gratitude. Well, the cook left, and retired some streets away to lodgings of her own; and there was Coolin in precisely the same situation with any young gentleman who has had the inestimable benefit of a faithful nurse. The canine conscience did not solve the problem with a pound of tea at Christmas. No longer content to pay a flying visit, it was the whole forenoon that he dedicated to his solitary friend. And so, day by day, he continued to comfort her solitude until (for some reason which I could never understand and cannot approve) he was kept locked up to break him of the graceful habit. Here, it is not the similarity, it is the difference, that is worthy of remark; the clearly marked degrees of gratitude and the proportional duration of his visits. Anything further removed from instinct it were hard to fancy; and one is even stirred to a certain impatience with a character so destitute of spontaneity, so passionless in justice, and so priggishly obedient to the voice of reason.

There are not many dogs like this good Coolin, and not many people. But the type is one well-marked, both in the human and the canine family. Gallantry was not his aim, but a solid and somewhat oppressive respectability. He was a sworn foe to the unusual and the conspicuous, a praiser of the golden mean, a kind of city uncle modified by Cheeryble. And as he was precise and conscientious in all the steps of his own blameless course, he looked for the same precision and an even greater gravity in the bearing of his deity, my father. It was no sinecure to be Coolin's idol: he was exacting like a rigid parent; and at every sign of levity in the man whom he respected, he announced loudly the death of virtue and the proximate fall of the pillars of the earth.

I have called him a snob; but all dogs are so, though in varying degrees. It is hard to follow their snobbery among themselves; for though I think we can perceive distinctions of rank, we cannot grasp what is the criterion. Thus in Edinburgh, in a good part of the town, there were several distinct societies or clubs that met in the morning to—the phrase is technical—to "rake the buckets" in a troop. A friend of mine, the master of three dogs, was one day surprised to observe that they had left one club and joined another; but whether it was a rise or a fall, and the result of an invitation or an expulsion, was more than he could guess. And this illustrates pointedly our ignorance of the real life of dogs, their social ambitions and their social hierarchies. At least, in their dealings with men they are not only conscious of sex, but of the difference of station. And that in the most snobbish manner: for the poor man's dog is not offended by the notice of the rich, and keeps all his ugly feeling for those poorer or more ragged than his master. And again, for every station they have an ideal of behaviour, to which the master, under pain of derogation, will do wisely to conform. How often has not a cold glance of an eye informed me that my dog was disappointed; and how much more gladly would he not have taken a beating than to be thus wounded in the seat of piety!

I knew one disrespectable dog. He was far liker a cat; cared little or nothing for men, with whom he merely co-existed as we do with cattle, and was entirely devoted to the art of poaching. A house would not hold him, and to live in a town was what he refused. He led, I believe, a life of troubled but genuine pleasure, and perished beyond all question in a trap. But this was an exception, a marked reversion to the ancestral type; like the hairy human infant. The true dog of the nineteenth century, to judge by the remainder of my fairly large acquaintance, is in love with respectability. A street-dog was once adopted by a lady. While still an Arab, he had done as Arabs do, gambolling in the mud, charging into butchers' stalls, a cat-hunter, a sturdy beggar, a common rogue and vagabond; but with his rise into society he laid aside these inconsistent pleasures. He stole no more, he hunted no more cats; and conscious of his collar, he ignored his old companions. Yet the canine upper class was never brought to recognise the upstart, and from that hour, except for human countenance, he was alone. Friendless, shorn of his sports and the habits of a lifetime, he still lived in a glory of happiness, content with his acquired respectability, and with no care but to support it solemnly. Are we to condemn or praise this self-made dog? We praise his human brother. And thus to conquer vicious habits is as rare with dogs as with men. With the more part, for all their scruple-mongering and moral thought, the vices that are born with them remain invincible throughout; and they live all their years, glorying in their virtues, but still the slaves of their defects. Thus the sage Coolin was a thief to the last; among a thousand peccadilloes, a whole goose and a whole cold leg of mutton lay upon his conscience; but Woggs,* whose soul's shipwreck in the matter of gallantry I have recounted above, has only twice been known to steal, and has often nobly conquered the temptation. The eighth is his favourite commandment. There is something painfully human in these unequal virtues and mortal frailties of the best. Still more painful is the bearing of those "stammering professors" in the house of sickness and under the terror of death. It is beyond a doubt to me that, somehow or

* Walter, Watty, Woggy, Woggs, Wogg, and lastly Bogue; under which last name he fell in battle some twelve months ago. Glory was his aim and he attained it; for his icon, by the hand of Caldecott, now lies among the treasures of the nation.

other, the dog connects together, or confounds, the uneasiness of sickness and the consciousness of guilt. To the pains of the body he often adds the tortures of the conscience; and at these times his haggard protestations form, in regard to the human deathbed, a dreadful parody or parallel.

I once supposed that I had found an inverse relation between the double etiquette which dogs obey; and that those who were most addicted to the showy street life among other dogs were less careful in the practice of home virtues for the tyrant man. But the female dog, that mass of carneying affectations, shines equally in either sphere; rules her rough posse of attendant swains with unwearying tact and gusto; and with her master and mistress pushes the arts of insinuation to their crowning point. The attention of man and the regard of other dogs flatter (it would thus appear) the same sensibility; but perhaps, if we could read the canine heart, they would be found to flatter it in very different degrees. Dogs live with man as courtiers round a monarch, steeped in the flattery of his notice and enriched with sinecures. To push their favour in this world of pickings and caresses is, perhaps, the business of their lives; and their joys may lie outside. I am in despair at our persistent ignorance. I read in the lives of our companions the same processes of reason, the same antique and fatal conflicts of the right against the wrong, and of unbitted nature with too rigid custom; I see them with our weaknesses, vain, false, inconstant against appetite, and with our one stalk of virtue, devoted to the dream of an ideal; and yet, as they hurry by me on the street with tail in air, or come singly to solicit my regard, I must own the secret purport of their lives is still inscrutable to man. Is man the friend, or is he the patron only? Have they indeed forgotten nature's voice? or are those moments snatched from courtiership when they touch noses with the tinker's mongrel, the brief reward and pleasure of their artificial lives? Doubtless, when man shares with his dog the toils of a profession and the pleasures of an art, as with the shepherd or the poacher, the affection warms and strengthens till it fills the soul. But doubtless, also, the masters are, in many cases, the object of a merely interested cultus, sitting aloft like Louis Quatorze, giving and receiving flattery and favour; and the dogs, like the majority of men, have but foregone their true existence and become the dupes of their ambition.

XIII

"A Penny Plain and Twopence Coloured"

THESE words will be familiar to all students of Skelt's Juvenile Drama. That national monument, after having changed its name to Park's, to Webb's, to Redington's, and last of all to Pollock's, has now become, for the most part, a memory. Some of its pillars, like Stonehenge, are still afoot, the rest clean vanished. It may be the Museum numbers a full set; and Mr. Ionides, perhaps, or else her gracious Majesty, may boast their great collections; but to the plain private person they are become, like Raphaels, unattainable. I have, at different times, possessed *Aladdin*, *The Red Rover*, *The Blind Boy*, *The Old Oak Chest*, *The Wood Dœmon*, *Jack Sheppard*, *The Miller and his Men*, *Der Freischütz*, *The Smuggler*, *The Forest of Bondy*, *Robin Hood*, *The Waterman*, *Richard I.*, *My Poll and my Partner Joe*, *The Inchcape Bell* (imperfect), and *Three-Fingered Jack, the Terror of Jamaica*; and I have assisted others in the illumination of *The Maid of the Inn* and *The Battle of Waterloo*. In this roll-call of stirring names you read the evidences of a happy childhood; and though not half of them are still to be procured of any living stationer, in the mind of their once happy owner all survive, kaleidoscopes of changing pictures, echoes of the past.

There stands, I fancy, to this day (but now how fallen!) a certain stationer's shop at a corner of the wide thoroughfare that joins the city of my childhood with the sea. When, upon any Saturday, we made a party to behold the ships, we passed that corner; and since in those days I loved a ship as a man loves Burgundy or daybreak, this of itself had been enough to hallow it. But there was more than that. In the Leith Walk window, all the year round, there stood displayed a theatre in working order, with a "forest set," a "combat," and a few "robbers carousing" in the slides; and below and about, dearer tenfold to me! the plays themselves, those budgets of romance, lay tumbled one upon another. Long and often have I lingered there with empty pockets. One figure, we shall say, was visible in the first plate of characters, bearded, pistol in hand, or drawing to his ear the clothyard arrow; I would spell the name: was it Macaire, or Long Tom Coffin, or Grindoff, 2d dress? O, how I would long to see the rest! how—if the name by chance were hidden—I would wonder in what play he figured, and what immortal legend justified his attitude and strange apparel! And then to go within, to announce yourself as an intending purchaser, and, closely watched, be suffered to undo those bundles and breathlessly devour those pages of gesticulating villains, epileptic combats, bosky forests, palaces and war-ships, frowning fortresses and prison vaults—it was a giddy joy. That shop, which was dark and smelt of Bibles, was a loadstone rock for all that bore the name of boy. They could not pass it by, nor, having entered, leave it. It was a place besieged; the shopmen, like the Jews rebuilding Salem, had a double task. They kept us at the stick's end, frowned us down, snatched each play out of our hand ere we were trusted with another; and, incredible as it may sound, used to demand of us upon our entrance, like banditti, if we came with money or with empty hand. Old Mr. Smith himself, worn out with my eternal vacillation, once swept the treasures from before me, with the cry: "I do not believe, child, that you are an intending purchaser at all!" These were the dragons of the garden; but for such joys of paradise we could have faced the Terror of Jamaica himself. Every sheet we fingered was another lightning glance into obscure, delicious story; it was like wallowing in the raw stuff of story-books. I know nothing to compare with it save now and then in dreams, when I am privileged to read in certain unwrit stories of adventure, from which I awake to find the world all vanity. The *crux* of Buridan's donkey was as nothing to the uncertainty of the boy as he handled and lingered and doated on these bundles of delight; there was a physical pleasure in the sight and touch of them which he would jealously prolong; and when at length the deed was done, the play selected, and the impatient shopman had brushed the rest into a gray portfolio, and the boy was forth again, a little late for dinner, the lamps springing into light in the blue winter's even, and *The Miller*, or *The Rover*, or some kindred drama clutched against his side—on what gay feet he ran, and how he laughed aloud in exultation! I can hear that laughter still. Out of all the years of my life, I can recall but one home-coming to compare with these, and that was on the night when I brought back with me the *Arabian Entertainments* in the fat, old, double-columned volume with the prints. I was just well into the story of the Hunchback, I remember, when my clergyman-grandfather (a man we counted pretty stiff) came in behind me. I grew blind with terror. But instead of ordering the book away, he said he envied me. Ah, well he might!

The purchase and the first half-hour at home, that was the summit. Thenceforth the interest declined by little and little. The fable, as set forth in the playbook, proved to be not worthy of the scenes and characters: what fable would not? Such passages as: "Scene 6. The Hermitage. Night set scene. Place back of scene 1, No. 2, at back of stage and hermitage, Fig. 2, out of set piece, R. H. in a slanting direction"—such passages, I say, though very practical, are hardly to be called good reading. Indeed, as literature, these dramas did not much appeal to me. I forget the very outline of the plots. Of *The Blind Boy*, beyond the fact that he was a most injured prince and once, I think, abducted, I know nothing. And *The Old Oak Chest*, what was it all about? that proscript (1st dress), that prodigious number of banditti, that old woman with the broom, and the magnificent kitchen in the third act (was it in the third?)—they are all fallen in a deliquium, swim faintly in my brain, and mix and vanish.

I cannot deny that joy attended the illumination; nor can I quite forget that child who, wilfully foregoing pleasure, stoops to "twopence coloured." With crimson lake (hark to the sound of it—crimson lake!—the horns of elf-land are not richer on the ear)—with crimson lake and Prussian blue a certain purple is to be compounded which, for cloaks especially, Titian could not equal. The latter colour with gamboge, a hated name although an exquisite pigment, supplied a green of such a savoury greenness that to-day my heart regrets it. Nor can I recall without a tender weakness the very aspect of the water where I dipped my brush. Yes, there was pleasure in the painting. But when all was painted, it is needless to deny it, all was spoiled. You might, indeed, set up a scene or two to look at; but to cut the figures out was simply sacrilege; nor could any child twice court the tedium, the worry, and the long-drawn disenchantment of an actual performance. Two days after the purchase the honey had been sucked. Parents used to complain; they thought I wearied of my play. It was not so: no more than a person can be said to have wearied of his dinner when he leaves the bones and dishes; I had got the marrow of it and said grace.

Then was the time to turn to the back of the playbook and to study that enticing double file of names, where poetry, for the true child of Skelt, reigned happy and glorious like her Majesty the Queen. Much as I have travelled in these realms of gold, I have yet seen, upon that map or abstract, names of El Dorados that still haunt the ear of memory, and are still but names. *The Floating Beacon*—why was that denied me? or *The Wreck Ashore? Sixteen-String Jack*, whom I did not even guess to be a highwayman, troubled me awake and haunted my slumbers; and there is one sequence of three from that enchanted calendar that I still at times recall, like a loved verse of poetry: *Lodoiska, Silver Palace, Echo of Westminster Bridge*. Names, bare names, are surely more to children than we poor, grown-up, obliterated fools remember.

The name of Skelt itself has always seemed a part and parcel of the charm of his productions. It may be different with the rose, but the attraction of this paper drama sensibly declined when Webb had crept into the rubric: a poor cuckoo, flaunting in Skelt's nest. And now we have reached Pollock, sounding deeper gulfs. Indeed, this name of Skelt appears so stagey and piratic, that I will adopt it boldly to design these qualities. Skeltery, then, is a quality of much art. It is even to be found, with reverence be it said, among the works of nature. The stagey is its generic name; but it is an old, insular, home-bred staginess; not French, domestically British; not of to-day, but smacking of O. Smith, Fitzball, and the great age of melodrama: a peculiar fragrance haunting it; uttering its unimportant message in a tone of voice that has the charm of fresh antiquity. I will not insist upon the art of Skelt's purveyors. These wonderful characters that once so thrilled our soul with their bold attitude, array of deadly engines and incomparable costume, to-day look somewhat pallidly; the extreme hard favour of the heroine strikes me, I had almost said with pain; the villain's scowl no longer thrills me like a trumpet; and the scenes themselves, those once unparalleled landscapes, seem the efforts of a prentice hand. So much of fault we find; but on the other side the impartial critic rejoices to remark the presence of a great unity of gusto; of those direct clap-trap appeals, which a man is dead and buriable when he fails to answer; of the footlight glamour, the ready-made, bare-faced, transpontine picturesque, a thing not one with cold reality, but how much dearer to the mind!

The scenery of Skeltdom—or, shall we say, the kingdom of Transpontus?—had a prevailing character. Whether it set forth Poland as in *The Blind Boy*, or Bohemia with *The Miller and his Men*, or Italy with *The Old Oak Chest*, still it was Transpontus. A botanist could tell it by the plants. The hollyhock was all pervasive, running wild in deserts; the dock was common, and the bending reed; and overshadowing these were poplar, palm, potato tree, and *Quercus Skeltica*—brave growths. The caves were all embowelled in the Surreyside formation; the soil was all betrodden by the light pump of T. P. Cooke. Skelt, to be sure, had yet another, an oriental string: he held the gorgeous East in fee; and in the new quarter of Hyères, say, in the garden of the Hotel des Iles d'Or, you may behold these blessed visions realised. But on these I will not dwell; they were an outwork; it was in the occidental scenery that Skelt was all himself. It had a strong flavour of England; it was a sort of indigestion of England and drop-scenes, and I am bound to say was charming. How the roads wander, how the castle sits upon the hill, how the sun eradiates from behind the cloud, and how the congregated clouds themselves uproll, as stiff as bolsters! Here is the cottage interior, the usual first flat, with the cloak upon the nail, the rosaries of onions, the gun and powder-horn and corner-cupboard; here is the inn (this drama must be nautical, I foresee Captain Luff and Bold Bob Bowsprit) with the red curtain, pipes, spittoons, and eight-day clock; and there again is that impressive dungeon with the chains, which was so dull to colour. England, the hedgerow elms, the thin brick houses, windmills, glimpses of the navigable Thames—England, when at last I came to visit it, was only Skelt made evident: to cross the border was, for the Scotsman, to come home to Skelt; there was the inn-sign and there the horse-trough, all foreshadowed in the faithful Skelt. If, at the ripe age of fourteen years, I bought a certain cudgel, got a friend to load it, and thenceforward walked the tame ways of the earth my own ideal, radiating pure romance—still I was but a puppet in the hand of Skelt; the original of that regretted bludgeon, and surely the antitype of all the bludgeon kind, greatly improved from Cruikshank, had adorned the hand of Jonathan Wild, pl. 1. "This is mastering me," as Whitman cries, upon some lesser provocation. What am I? what are life, art, letters, the world, but what my Skelt has made them? He stamped himself upon my immaturity. The world was plain before I knew him, a poor penny world; but soon it was all coloured with romance. If I go to the theatre to see a good old melodrama, 'tis but Skelt a little faded. If I visit a bold scene in nature, Skelt would have been bolder; there had been certainly a castle on that mountain, and the hollow tree—that set piece—I seem to miss it in the foreground. Indeed, out of this cut-and-dry, dull, swaggering, obtrusive, and infantile art, I seem to have learned the very spirit of my life's enjoyment; met there the shadows of the characters I was to read about and love in a late future; got the romance of *Der Freischütz* long ere I was to hear of Weber or the mighty Formes; acquired a gallery of scenes and characters with which, in the silent theatre of the brain, I might enact all novels and romances; and took from these rude cuts an enduring and transforming pleasure. Reader—and yourself?

A word of moral: it appears that B. Pollock, late J. Redington, No. 73 Hoxton Street, not only publishes twenty-three of these old stage favourites, but owns the necessary plates and displays a modest readiness to issue other thirty-three. If you love art, folly, or the bright eyes of children, speed to Pollock's, or to Clarke's of Garrick Street. In Pollock's list of publicanda I perceive a pair of my ancient aspirations: *Wreck Ashore* and *Sixteen-String Jack;* and I cherish the belief that when these shall see once more the light of day, B. Pollock will remember this apologist. But, indeed, I have a dream at times that is not all a dream. I seem to myself to wander in a ghostly street—E. W., I think, the postal district—close below the fool's-cap of St. Paul's and yet within easy hearing of the echo of the Abbey bridge. There is a dim shop, low in the roof and smelling strong of glue and footlights, I find myself in quaking treaty with great Skelt himself, the aboriginal, all dusty from the tomb. I buy, with what a choking heart—I buy them all, all but the pantomimes; I pay my mental money, and go forth; and lo! the packets are dust.

XIV

A Gossip on a Novel of Dumas's

THE books that we re-read the oftenest are not always those that we admire the most; we choose and we revisit them for many and various reasons, as we choose and revisit human friends. One or two of Scott's novels, Shakespeare, Molière, Montaigne, *The Egoist*, and the *Vicomte de Bragelonne*, form the inner circle of my intimates. Behind these comes a good troop of dear acquaintances; *The Pilgrim's Progress* in the front rank, *The Bible in Spain* not far behind. There are besides a certain number that look at me with reproach as I pass them by on my shelves: books that I once thumbed and studied: houses which were once like home to me, but where I now rarely visit. I am on these sad terms (and blush to confess it) with Wordsworth, Horace, Burns and Hazlitt. Last of all, there is the class of book that has its hour of brilliancy—glows, sings, charms, and then fades again into insignificance until the fit return. Chief of those who thus smile and frown on me by turns, I must name Virgil and Herrick, who, were they but

"Their sometime selves the same throughout the year,"

must have stood in the first company with the six names of my continual literary intimates. To these six, incongruous as they seem, I have long been faithful, and hope to be faithful to the day of death. I have never read the whole of Montaigne, but I do not like to be long without reading some of him, and my delight in what I do read never lessens. Of Shakespeare I have read all but *Richard III.*, *Henry VI.*, *Titus Andronicus*, and *All's Well that Ends Well*; and these, having already made all suitable endeavour, I now know that I shall never read—to make up for which unfaithfulness I could read much of the rest for ever. Of Molière—surely the next greatest name of Christendom—I could tell a very similar story; but in a little corner of a little essay these princes are too much out of place, and I prefer to pay my fealty and pass on. How often I have read *Guy Mannering*, *Rob Roy*, or *Redgauntlet*, I have no means of guessing, having begun young. But it is either four or five times that I have read *The Egoist*, and either five or six that I have read the *Vicomte de Bragelonne*.

Some, who would accept the others, may wonder that I should have spent so much of this brief life of ours over a work so little famous as the last. And, indeed, I am surprised myself; not at my own devotion, but the coldness of the world. My acquaintance with the *Vicomte* began, somewhat indirectly, in the year of grace 1863, when I had the advantage of studying certain illustrated dessert plates in a hotel at Nice.

The name of d'Artagnan in the legends I already saluted like an old friend, for I had met it the year before in a work of Miss Yonge's. My first perusal was in one of those pirated editions that swarmed at that time out of Brussels, and ran to such a troop of neat and dwarfish volumes. I understood but little of the merits of the book; my strongest memory is of the execution of d'Eyméric and Lyodot—a strange testimony to the dulness of a boy, who could enjoy the rough-and-tumble in the Place de Grêve, and forget d'Artagnan's visits to the two financiers. My next reading was in winter-time, when I lived alone upon the Pentlands. I would return in the early night from one of my patrols with the shepherd; a friendly face would meet me in the door, a friendly retriever scurry upstairs to fetch my slippers; and I would sit down with the *Vicomte* for a long, silent, solitary lamp-light evening by the fire. And yet I know not why I call it silent, when it was enlivened with such a clatter of horse-shoes, and such a rattle of musketry, and such a stir of talk; or why I call those evenings solitary in which I gained so many friends. I would rise from my book and pull the blind aside, and see the snow and the glittering hollies chequer a Scotch garden, and the winter moonlight brighten the white hills. Thence I would turn again to that crowded and sunny field of life in which it was so easy to forget myself, my cares, and my surroundings: a place busy as a city, bright as a theatre, thronged with memorable faces, and sounding with delightful speech. I carried the thread of that epic into my slumbers, I woke with it unbroken, I rejoiced to plunge into the book again at breakfast, it was with a pang that I must lay it down and turn to my own labours; for no part of the world has ever seemed to me so charming as these pages, and not even my friends are quite so real, perhaps quite so dear, as d'Artagnan.

Since then I have been going to and fro at very brief intervals in my favourite book; and I have now just risen from my last (let me call it my fifth) perusal, having liked it better and admired it more seriously than ever. Perhaps I have a sense of ownership, being so well known in these six volumes. Perhaps I think that d'Artagnan delights to have me read of him, and Louis Quatorze is gratified and Fouquet throws me a look, and Aramis, although he knows I do not love him, yet plays to me with his best graces, as to an old patron of the show. Perhaps, if I am not careful, something may befall me like what befell George IV. about the battle of Waterloo, and I may come to fancy the *Vicomte* one of the first, and Heaven knows the best, of my own works. At least, I avow myself a partisan; and when I compare the popularity of the *Vicomte* with that of *Monte Cristo*, or its own elder brother, the *Trois Mousquetaires*, I confess I am both pained and puzzled.

To those who have already made acquaintance with the titular hero in the pages of *Vingt Ans*

Après, perhaps the name may act as a deterrent. A man might well stand back if he supposed he were to follow, for six volumes, so well-conducted, so fine-spoken, and withal so dreary a cavalier as Bragelonne. But the fear is idle. I may be said to have passed the best years of my life in these six volumes, and my acquaintance with Raoul has never gone beyond a bow; and when he, who has so long pretended to be alive, is at last suffered to pretend to be dead, I am sometimes reminded of a saying in an earlier volume: "*Enfin, dit Miss Stewart*,"—and it was of Bragelonne she spoke—"*enfin il a fait quelque-chose: c'est, ma foi! bien heureux*." I am reminded of it, as I say; and the next moment, when Athos dies of his death, and my dear d'Artagnan bursts into his storms of sobbing, I can but deplore my flippancy.

Or perhaps it is La Vallière that the reader of *Vingt Ans Après* is inclined to flee. Well, he is right there too, though not so right. Louise is no success. Her creator has spared no pains; she is well-meant, not ill-designed, sometimes has a word that rings out true; sometimes, if only for a breath, she may even engage our sympathies. But I have never envied the King his triumph. And so far from pitying Bragelonne for his defeat, I could wish him no worse (not for lack of malice, but imagination) than to be wedded to that lady. Madame enchants me; I can forgive that royal minx her most serious offences; I can thrill and soften with the King on that memorable occasion when he goes to upbraid and remains to flirt; and when it comes to the "*Allons, aimez-moi donc,*" it is my heart that melts in the bosom of de Guiche. Not so with Louise. Readers cannot fail to have remarked that what an author tells us of the beauty of the charm of his creatures goes for nought; that we know instantly better; that the heroine cannot open her mouth but what, all in a moment, the fine phrases of preparation fall from round her like the robes from Cinderella, and she stands before us, self-betrayed, as a poor, ugly, sickly wench, or perhaps a strapping market-woman. Authors, at least, know it well; a heroine will too often start the trick of "getting ugly"; and no disease is more difficult to cure. I said authors; but indeed I had a side eye to one author in particular, with whose works I am very well acquainted, though I cannot read them, and who has spent many vigils in this cause, sitting beside his ailing puppets and (like a magician) wearying his art to restore them to youth and beauty. There are others who ride too high for these misfortunes. Who doubts the loveliness of Rosalind? Arden itself was not more lovely. Who ever questioned the perennial charm of Rose Jocelyn, Lucy Desborough, or Clara Middleton? fair women with fair names, the daughters of George Meredith. Elizabeth Bennet has but to speak, and I am at her knees. Ah! these are the creators of desirable women. They would never have fallen in the mud with Dumas and poor

La Vallière. It is my only consolation that not one of all of them, except the first, could have plucked at the moustache of d'Artagnan.

Or perhaps, again, a proportion of readers stumble at the threshold. In so vast a mansion there were sure to be back stairs and kitchen offices where no one would delight to linger; but it was at least unhappy that the vestibule should be so badly lighted; and until, in the seventeenth chapter, d'Artagnan sets off to seek his friends, I must confess, the book goes heavily enough. But, from thenceforward, what a feast is spread! Monk kidnapped; d'Artagnan enriched; Mazarin's death; the ever delectable adventure of Belle Isle, wherein Aramis outwits d'Artagnan, with its epilogue (vol. v. chap. xxviii.), where d'Artagnan regains the moral superiority; the love adventures at Fontainebleau, with St. Aignan's story of the dryad and the business of de Guiche, de Wardes, and Manicamp; Aramis made general of the Jesuits; Aramis at the bastille; the night talk in the forest of Sénart; Belle Isle again, with the death of Porthos; and last, but not least, the taming of d'Artagnan the untamable, under the lash of the young King. What other novel has such epic variety and nobility of incident? often, if you will, impossible; often of the order of an Arabian story; and yet all based in human nature. For if you come to that, what novel has more human nature? not studied with the microscope, but seen largely, in plain daylight, with the natural eye? What novel has more good sense, and gaiety, and wit, and unflagging, admirable literary skill? Good souls, I suppose, must sometimes read it in the blackguard travesty of a translation. But there is no style so untranslatable; light as a whipped trifle, strong as silk; wordy like a village tale; pat like a general's despatch; with every fault, yet never tedious; with no merit, yet inimitably right. And, once more, to make an end of commendations, what novel is inspired with a more unstrained or a more wholesome morality?

Yes; in spite of Miss Yonge, who introduced me to the name of d'Artagnan only to dissuade me from a nearer knowledge of the man, I have to add morality. There is no quite good book without a good morality; but the world is wide, and so are morals. Out of two people who have dipped into Sir Richard Burton's *Thousand and One Nights*, one shall have been offended by the animal details; another to whom these were harmless, perhaps even pleasing, shall yet have been shocked in his turn by the rascality and cruelty of all the characters. Of two readers, again, one shall have been pained by the morality of a religious memoir, one by that of the *Vicomte de Bragelonne*. And the point is that neither need be wrong. We shall always shock each other both in life and art; we cannot get the sun into our pictures, nor the abstract right (if there be such a thing) into our books; enough if, in the one, there glimmer some hint of the great light that blinds us from heaven; enough if, in the other, there shine, even upon foul details, a spirit of magnanimity. I would scarce send to the *Vicomte* a reader who was in quest of what we may call puritan morality. The ventripotent mulatto, the great eater, worker, earner and waster, the man of much and witty laughter, the man of the great heart and alas! of the doubtful honesty, is a figure not yet clearly set before the world; he still awaits a sober and yet genial portrait; but with whatever art that may be touched, and whatever indulgence, it will not be the portrait of a precisian. Dumas was certainly not thinking of himself, but of Planchet, when he put into the mouth of d'Artagnan's old servant this excellent profession: "*Monsieur, j'étais une de ces bonnes pâtes d'hommes que Dieu a fait pour s'animer pendant un certain temps et pour trouver bonnes toutes choses qui accompagnent leur séjour sur la terre.*" He was thinking, as I say, of Planchet, to whom the words are aptly fitted; but they were fitted also to Planchet's creator; and perhaps this struck him as he wrote, for observe what follows: "*D'Artagnan s'assit alors près de la fenêtre, et, cette philosophie de Planchet lui ayant paru solide, il y rêva.*" In a man who finds all things good, you will scarce expect much zeal for negative virtues: the active alone will have a charm for him; abstinence, however wise, however kind, will always seem to such a judge entirely mean and partly impious. So with

Dumas. Chastity is not near his heart; nor yet, to his own sore cost, that virtue of frugality which is the armour of the artist. Now, in the *Vicomte*, he had much to do with the contest of Fouquet and Colbert. Historic justice should be all upon the side of Colbert, of official honesty, and fiscal competence. And Dumas knew it well: three times at least he shows his knowledge; once it is but flashed upon us and received with the laughter of Fouquet himself, in the jesting controversy in the gardens of Saint Mandé; once it is touched on by Aramis in the forest of Sénart; in the end, it is set before us clearly in one dignified speech of the triumphant Colbert. But in Fouquet, the waster, the lover of good cheer and wit and art, the swift transactor of much business, "*l'homme de bruit, l'homme de plaisir, l'homme qui n'est que parceque les autres sont,*" Dumas saw something of himself and drew the figure the more tenderly. It is to me even touching to see how he insists on Fouquet's honour; not seeing, you might think, that unflawed honour is impossible to spendthrifts; but rather, perhaps, in the light of his own life, seeing it too well, and clinging the more to what was left. Honour can survive a wound; it can live and thrive without a member. The man rebounds from his disgrace; he begins fresh foundations on the ruins of the old; and when his sword is broken, he will do valiantly with his dagger. So it is with Fouquet in the book; so it was with Dumas on the battlefield of life.

To cling to what is left of any damaged quality is virtue in the man; but perhaps to sing its praises is scarcely to be called morality in the writer. And it is elsewhere, it is in the character of d'Artagnan, that we must look for that spirit of morality, which is one of the chief merits of the book, makes one of the main joys of its perusal, and sets it high above more popular rivals. Athos, with the coming of years, has declined too much into the preacher, and the preacher of a sapless creed; but d'Artagnan has mellowed into a man so witty, rough, kind and upright, that he takes the heart by storm. There is nothing of the copy-book about his virtues, nothing of the drawing-room in his fine, natural civility; he will sail near the wind; he is no district visitor—no Wesley or Robespierre; his conscience is void of all refinement whether for good or evil; but the whole man rings true like a good sovereign. Readers who have approached the *Vicomte*, not across country, but by the legitimate, five-volumed avenue of the *Mousquetaires* and *Vingt Ans Après*, will not have forgotten d'Artagnan's ungentlemanly and perfectly improbable trick upon Milady. What a pleasure it is, then, what a reward, and how agreeable a lesson, to see the old captain humble himself to the son of the man whom he had personated! Here, and throughout, if I am to choose virtues for myself or my friends, let me choose the virtues of d'Artagnan. I do not say there is no character as well drawn in Shakespeare; I do say there is none that I love so wholly. There are many spiritual eyes that seem to spy upon our actions—eyes of the dead and the absent, whom we imagine to behold us in our most private hours, and whom we fear and scruple to offend: our witnesses and judges. And among these, even if you should think me childish, I must count my d'Artagnan—not d'Artagnan of the memoirs whom Thackeray pretended to prefer—a preference, I take the freedom of saying, in which he stands alone; not the d'Artagnan of flesh and blood, but him of the ink and paper; not Nature's, but Dumas's. And this is the particular crown and triumph of the artist—not to be true merely, but to be lovable; not simply to convince, but to enchant.

There is yet another point in the *Vicomte* which I find incomparable. I can recall no other work of the imagination in which the end of life is represented with so nice a tact. I was asked the other day if Dumas made me laugh or cry. Well, in this my late fifth reading of the *Vicomte*, I did laugh once at the small Coquelin de Volière business, and was perhaps a thought surprised at having done so: to make up for it, I smiled continually. But for tears, I do not know. If you put a pistol to my throat, I must own the tale trips upon a very airy foot—within a measurable distance of unreality; and for those who like the big guns to be discharged and the great passions to appear authentically, it may even seem inadequate from first to last. Not so to me ; I cannot count that a poor dinner, or a poor book, where I meet with those I love ; and, above all, in this last volume, I find a singular charm of spirit. It breathes a pleasant and a tonic sadness, always brave, never hysterical. Upon the crowded, noisy life of this long tale, evening gradually falls ; and the lights are extinguished, and the heroes pass away one by one. One by one they go, and not a regret embitters their departure ; the young succeed them in their places, Louis Quatorze is swelling larger and shining broader, another generation and another France dawn on the horizon ; but for us and these old men whom we have loved so long, the inevitable end draws near and is welcome. To read this well is to anticipate experience. Ah, if only when these hours of the long shadows fall for us in reality and not in figure, we may hope to face them with a mind as quiet !

But my paper is running out ; the siege guns are firing on the Dutch frontier ; and I must say adieu for the fifth time to my old comrade fallen on the field of glory. *Adieu*—rather *au revoir !* Yet a sixth time, dearest d'Artagnan, we shall kidnap Monk and take horse together for Belle Isle.

XV

A Gossip on Romance

IN anything fit to be called by the name of reading, the process itself should be absorbing and voluptuous; we should gloat over a book, be rapt clean out of ourselves, and rise from the perusal, our mind filled with the busiest, kaleidoscopic dance of images, incapable of sleep or of continuous thought. The words, if the book be eloquent, should run thenceforward in our ears like the noise of breakers, and the story, if it be a story, repeat itself in a thousand coloured pictures to the eye. It was for this last pleasure that we read so closely, and loved our books so dearly, in the bright, troubled period of boyhood. Eloquence and thought, character and conversation, were but obstacles to brush aside as we dug blithely after a certain sort of incident, like a pig for truffles. For my part, I liked a story to begin with an old wayside inn where, "towards the close of the year 17—," several gentlemen in three-cocked hats were playing bowls. A friend of mine preferred the Malabar coast in a storm, with a ship beating to windward, and a scowling fellow of Herculean proportions striding along the beach ; he, to be sure, was a pirate. This was further afield than my home-keeping fancy loved to travel, and designed altogether for a larger canvas than the tales that I affected. Give me a highwayman and I was full to the brim ; a Jacobite would do, but the highwayman was my favourite dish. I can still hear that merry clatter of the hoofs along the moonlit lane ; night and the coming of day are still related in my mind with the doings of John Rann or Jerry Abershaw ; and the words "post-chaise," the "great North Road," "ostler," and "nag" still sound in my ears like poetry. One and all, at least, and each with his particular fancy, we read story-books in childhood, not for eloquence or character or thought, but for some quality of the brute incident. That quality was not mere bloodshed or wonder. Although each of these was welcome in its place, the charm for the sake of which we read depended on something different from either. My elders used to read novels aloud ; and I can still remember four different passages which I heard, before I was ten, with the same keen and lasting pleasure. One I discovered long afterwards to be the admirable opening of *What will he Do with It:* it was no wonder I was pleased with that. The other three still remain unidentified. One is a little vague ; it was about a dark, tall house at night, and people groping on the stairs by the light that escaped from the open door of a sickroom. In another, a lover left a ball, and went walking in a cool, dewy park, whence he could watch the lighted windows and the figures of the dancers as they moved. This was the most sentimental impression I think I had yet received, for a child is somewhat deaf to the sentimental. In the last, a poet, who had been tragically wrangling with his wife, walked forth on the sea-beach on a tempestuous night and witnessed the horrors of a wreck.* Different as they are, all these early favourites have a common note—they have all a touch of the romantic.

Drama is the poetry of conduct, romance the poetry of circumstance. The pleasure that we take in life is of two sorts—the active and the passive. Now we are conscious of a great command over our destiny; anon we are lifted up by circumstance, as by a breaking wave, and dashed we know not how into the future. Now we are pleased by our conduct, anon merely pleased by our surroundings. It would be hard to say which of these modes of satisfaction is the more effective, but the latter is surely the more constant. Conduct is three-parts of life, they say; but I think they put it high. There is a vast deal in life and letters both which is not immoral, but simply a-moral; which either does not regard the human will at all, or deals with it in obvious and healthy relations; where the interest turns, not upon what a man shall choose to do, but on how he manages to do it; not on the passionate slips and hesitations of the con-

* Since traced by many obliging correspondents to the gallery of Charles Kingsley.

science, but on the problems of the body and of the practical intelligence, in clean, open-air adventure, the shock of arms or the diplomacy of life. With such material as this it is impossible to build a play, for the serious theatre exists solely on moral grounds, and is a standing proof of the dissemination of the human conscience. But it is possible to build, upon this ground, the most joyous of verses, and the most lively, beautiful, and buoyant tales.

One thing in life calls for another; there is a fitness in events and places. The sight of a pleasant arbour puts it in our mind to sit there. One place suggests work, another idleness, a third early rising and long rambles in the dew. The effect of night, of any flowing water, of lighted cities, of the peep of day, of ships, of the open ocean, calls up in the mind an army of anonymous desires and pleasures. Something, we feel, should happen; we know not what, yet we proceed in quest of it. And many of the happiest hours of life fleet by us in this vain attendance on the genius of the place and moment. It is thus that tracts of young fir, and low rocks that reach into deep soundings, particularly torture and delight me. Something must have happened in such places, and perhaps ages back, to members of my race; and when I was a child I tried in vain to invent appropriate games for them, as I still try, just as vainly, to fit them with the proper story. Some places speak distinctly. Certain dank gardens cry aloud for a murder; certain old houses demand to be haunted; certain coasts are set apart for shipwreck. Other spots again seem to abide their destiny, suggestive and impenetrable, "miching mallecho." The inn at Burford Bridge, with its arbours and green garden and silent, eddying river—though it is known already as the place where Keats wrote some of his *Endymion* and Nelson parted from his Emma—still seems to wait the coming of the appropriate legend. Within these ivied walls, behind these old green shutters, some further business smoulders, waiting for its hour. The old Hawes Inn at the Queen's Ferry makes a similar call upon my fancy. There it stands, apart from the town, beside the pier, in a climate of its own, half inland, half marine—in front, the ferry bubbling with the tide and the guardship swinging to her anchor; behind, the old garden with the trees. Americans seek it already for the sake of Lovel and Oldbuck, who dined there at the beginning of the *Antiquary*. But you need not tell me—that is not all; there is some story, unrecorded or not yet complete, which must express the meaning of that inn more fully. So it is with names and faces; so it is with incidents that are idle and inconclusive in themselves, and yet seem like the beginning of some quaint romance, which the all-careless author leaves untold. How many of these romances have we not seen determine at their birth; how many people have met us with a look of meaning in their eye, and sunk at once into trivial acquaintances; to how many places have we not drawn near, with express intimations—"here my destiny awaits me"—and we have but dined there and passed on! I have lived both at the Hawes and Burford in a perpetual flutter, on the heels, as it seemed, of some adventure that should justify the place; but though the feeling had me to bed at night and called me again at morning in one unbroken round of pleasure and suspense, nothing befell me in either worth remark. The man or the hour had not yet come; but some day, I think, a boat shall put off from the Queen's Ferry, fraught with a dear cargo, and some frosty night a horseman, on a tragic errand, rattle with his whip upon the green shutters of the inn at Burford.*

Now, this is one of the natural appetites with which any lively literature has to count. The desire for knowledge, I had almost added the desire for meat, is not more deeply seated than this demand for fit and striking incident. The dullest of clowns tells, or tries to tell, himself a story, as the feeblest of children uses invention in his play; and even as the imaginative grown person, joining in the game, at once enriches it with many delightful circumstances, the great creative writer shows us the realisation and the apotheosis of the day-dreams of common men. His stories may be nourished with the realities of

* Since the above was written I have tried to launch the boat with my own hands in *Kidnapped.* Some day, perhaps, I may try a rattle at the shutters.

life, but their true mark is to satisfy the nameless longings of the reader, and to obey the ideal laws of the day-dream. The right kind of thing should fall out in the right kind of place; the right kind of thing should follow; and not only the characters talk aptly and think naturally, but all the circumstances in a tale answer one to another like notes in music. The threads of a story come from time to time together and make a picture in the web; the characters fall from time to time into some attitude to each other or to nature, which stamps the story home like an illustration. Crusoe recoiling from the footprint, Achilles shouting over against the Trojans, Ulysses bending the great bow, Christian running with his fingers in his ears, these are each culminating moments in the legend, and each has been printed on the mind's eye for ever. Other things we may forget; we may forget the words, although they are beautiful; we may forget the author's comment, although perhaps it was ingenious and true; but these epoch-making scenes, which put the last mark of truth upon a story and fill up, at one blow, our capacity for sympathetic pleasure, we so adopt into the very bosom of our mind that neither time nor tide can efface or weaken the impression. This, then, is the plastic part of literature: to embody character, thought, or emotion in some act or attitude that shall be remarkably striking to the mind's eye. This is the highest and hardest thing to do in words; the thing which, once accomplished, equally delights the schoolboy and the sage, and makes, in its own right, the quality of epics. Compared with this, all other purposes in literature, except the purely lyrical or the purely philosophic, are bastard in nature, facile of execution, and feeble in result. It is one thing to write about the inn at Burford, or to describe scenery with the word-painters; it is quite another to seize on the heart of the suggestion and make a country famous with a legend. It is one thing to remark and to dissect, with the most cutting logic, the complications of life, and of the human spirit; it is quite another to give them body and blood in the story of Ajax or of Hamlet. The first is literature, but the second is something besides, for it is likewise art.

English people of the present day * are apt, I know not why, to look somewhat down on incident, and reserve their admiration for the clink of teaspoons and the accents of the curate. It is thought clever to write a novel with no story at all, or at least with a very dull one. Reduced even to the lowest terms, a certain interest can be communicated by the art of narrative; a sense of human kinship is stirred; and a kind of monotonous fitness, comparable to the words and air of *Sandy's Mull*, preserved among the infinitesimal occurrences recorded. Some people work, in this manner, with even a strong touch. Mr. Trollope's inimitable clergymen naturally arise to the mind in this connec-

* 1882.

tion. But even Mr. Trollope does not confine himself to chronicling small beer. Mr. Crawley's collision with the Bishop's wife, Mr. Melnotte dallying in the deserted banquet-room, are typical incidents, epically conceived, fitly embodying a crisis. Or again look at Thackeray. If Rawdon Crawley's blow were not delivered, *Vanity Fair* would cease to be a work of art. That scene is the chief ganglion of the tale; and the discharge of energy from Rawdon's fist is the reward and consolation of the reader. The end of *Esmond* is a yet wider excursion from the author's customary fields; the scene at Castlewood is pure Dumas; the great and wily English borrower has here borrowed from the great, unblushing French thief; as usual, he has borrowed admirably well, and the breaking of the sword rounds off the best of all his books with a manly, martial note. But perhaps nothing can more strongly illustrate the necessity for marking incident than to compare the living fame of *Robinson Crusoe* with the discredit of *Clarissa Harlowe*. *Clarissa* is a book of a far more startling import, worked out, on a great canvas, with inimitable courage and unflagging art. It contains wit, character, passion, plot, conversations full of spirit and insight, letters sparkling with unrestrained humanity; and if the death of the heroine be somewhat frigid and artificial the last days of the hero strike the only note of what we now call Byronism, between the Elizabethans and Byron himself. And yet a little story of a shipwrecked sailor, with not a tenth part of the style nor a thousandth part of the wisdom, exploring none of the arcana of humanity and deprived of the perennial interest of love, goes on from edition to edition, ever young, while *Clarissa* lies upon the shelves unread. A friend of mine, a Welsh blacksmith, was twenty-five years old and could neither read nor write, when he heard a chapter of *Robinson* read aloud in a farm kitchen. Up to that moment he had sat content, huddled in his ignorance, but he left that farm another man. There were day-dreams, it appeared, divine day-dreams, written and printed and bound, and to be bought for money and enjoyed at pleasure. Down he sat that day, painfully learned to read Welsh, and returned to borrow the book. It had been lost, nor could he find another copy but one that was in English. Down he sat once more, learned English, and at length, and with entire delight, read *Robinson*. It is like the story of a love-chase. If he had heard a letter from *Clarissa*, would he have been fired with the same chivalrous ardour ? I wonder. Yet *Clarissa* has every quality that can be shown in prose, one alone excepted—pictorial or picture-making romance. While *Robinson* depends, for the most part and with the overwhelming majority of its readers, on the charm of circumstance.

In the highest achievements of the art of words, the dramatic and the pictorial, the moral and romantic interest, rise and fall together by a common and organic law. Situation is animated with passion, passion clothed upon with situation. Neither exists for itself, but each inheres indissolubly with the other. This is high art; and not only the highest art possible in words, but the highest art of all, since it combines the greatest mass and diversity of the elements of truth and pleasure. Such are epics, and the few prose tales that have the epic weight. But as from a school of works, aping the creative, incident and romance are ruthlessly discarded, so may character and drama be omitted or subordinated to romance. There is one book, for example, more generally loved than Shakespeare, that captivates in childhood, and still delights in age—I mean the *Arabian Nights*—where you shall look in vain for moral or for intellectual interest. No human face or voice greets us among that wooden crowd of kings and genies, sorcerers and beggarmen. Adventure, on the most naked terms, furnishes forth the entertainment and is found enough. Dumas approaches perhaps nearest of any modern to these Arabian authors in the purely material charm of some of his romances. The early part of *Monte Cristo*, down to the finding of the treasure, is a piece of perfect story-telling; the man never breathed who shared these moving incidents without a tremor; and yet Faria is a thing of packthread and Dantès little more than a name. The sequel is one long-drawn error, gloomy, bloody, unnatural and dull; but as for these early chapters, I do not believe there is another volume extant where you can breathe the same unmingled atmosphere of romance. It is very thin and light, to be sure, as on a high mountain; but it is brisk and clear and sunny in proportion. I saw the other day, with envy, an old and a very clever lady setting forth on a second or third voyage into *Monte Cristo*. Here are stories which powerfully affect the reader, which can be reperused at any age, and where the characters are no more than puppets. The bony fist of the showman visibly propels them; their springs are an open secret; their faces are of wood, their bellies filled with bran; and yet we thrillingly partake of their adventures. And the point may be illustrated still further. The last interview between Lucy and Richard Feveril is pure drama; more than that, it is the strongest scene, since Shakespeare, in the English tongue. Their first meeting by the river, on the other hand, is pure romance; it has nothing to do with character; it might happen to any other boy or maiden, and be none the less delightful for the change. And yet I think he would be a bold man who should choose between these passages. Thus, in the same book, we may have two scenes, each capital in its order: in the one, human passion, deep calling unto deep, shall utter its genuine voice; in the second, according circumstances, like instruments in tune, shall build up a trivial but desirable incident, such as we love to prefigure for ourselves; and in the end, in spite of the critics, we may hesitate to give the preference to either. The one may ask more genius—I do not say it does; but at least the other dwells as clearly in the memory.

True romantic art, again, makes a romance of all things. It reaches into the highest abstraction of the ideal; it does not refuse the most pedestrian realism. *Robinson Crusoe* is as realistic as it is romantic; both qualities are pushed to an extreme, and neither suffers. Nor does romance depend upon the material importance of the incidents. To deal with strong and deadly elements, banditti, pirates, war and murder, is to conjure with great names, and, in the event of failure, to double the disgrace. The arrival of Haydn and Consuelo at the Canon's villa is a very trifling incident; yet we may read a dozen boisterous stories from beginning to end, and not receive so fresh and stirring an impression of adventure. It was the scene of Crusoe at the wreck, if I remember rightly, that so bewitched my blacksmith. Nor is the fact surprising. Every single article the castaway recovers from the hulk is "a joy for ever" to the man who reads of them. They are the things that should be found, and the bare enumeration stirs the blood. I found a glimmer of the same interest the other day in a new book, *The Sailor's Sweetheart*, by Mr. Clark Russell. The whole business of the brig *Morning Star* is very rightly felt and spiritedly written; but the clothes, the books and the money satisfy the reader's mind like things to eat. We are dealing here with the old cut-and-dry, legitimate interest of treasure trove. But even treasure trove can be made dull. There are few people who have not groaned under the plethora of goods that fell to the lot of the *Swiss Family Robinson*, that dreary family. They found article after article, creature after creature, from milk kine to pieces of ordnance, a whole consignment; but no informing taste had presided over the selection, there was no smack or relish in the invoice; and these riches left the fancy cold. The box of goods in Verne's *Mysterious Island* is another case in point: there was no gusto and no glamour about that; it might have come from a shop. But the two hundred and seventy-eight Australian sovereigns on board the *Morning Star* fell upon me like a surprise that I had expected; whole vistas of secondary stories, besides the one in hand, radiated forth from that discovery, as they radiate from a striking particular in life; and I was made for the moment as happy as a reader has the right to be.

To come at all at the nature of this quality of romance, we must bear in mind the peculiarity of our attitude to any art. No art produces illusion; in the theatre we never forget that we are in the theatre; and while we read a story, we sit wavering between two minds, now merely clapping our hands at the merit of the performance, now condescending to take an active part in fancy with the characters. This last is the triumph of romantic story-telling: when the reader consciously plays at being the hero, the scene is a good scene. Now in character-studies the pleasure that we take is critical; we watch, we approve, we smile at incongruities, we are moved to sudden heats of sympathy with courage, suffering or virtue. But the characters are still themselves, they are not us; the more clearly they are depicted, the more widely do they stand away from us, the more imperiously do they thrust us back into our place as a spectator. I cannot identify myself with Rawdon Crawley or with Eugène de Rastignac, for I have scarce a hope or fear in common with them. It is not character but incident that woos us out of our reserve. Something happens as we desire to have it happen to ourselves; some situation, that we have long dallied with in fancy, is realised in the story with enticing and appropriate details. Then we forget the characters; then we push the hero aside; then we plunge into the tale in our own person and bathe in fresh experience; and then, and then only, do we say we have been reading a romance. It is not only pleasurable things that we imagine in our day-dreams; there are lights in which we are willing to contemplate even the idea of our own death; ways in which it seems as if it would amuse us to be cheated, wounded or calumniated. It is thus possible to construct a story, even of tragic import, in which every incident, detail and trick of circumstance shall be welcome to the reader's thoughts. Fiction is to the grown man what play is to the child; it is there that he changes the atmosphere and tenor of his life; and when the game so chimes with his fancy that he can join in it with all his heart, when it pleases him with every turn, when he loves to recall it and dwells upon its recollection with entire delight, fiction is called romance.

Walter Scott is out and away the king of the romantics. *The Lady of the Lake* has no indisputable claim to be a poem beyond the inherent fitness and desirability of the tale. It is just such a story as a man would make up for himself, walking, in the best health and temper, through just such scenes as it is laid in. Hence it is that a charm dwells undefinable among these slovenly verses, as the unseen cuckoo fills the mountains with his note; hence, even after we have flung the book aside, the scenery and adventures remain present to the mind, a new and green possession, not unworthy of that beautiful name, *The Lady of the Lake*, or that direct, romantic opening—one of the most spirited and poetical in literature—"The stag at eve had drunk his fill." The same strength and the same weaknesses adorn and disfigure the novels. In that ill-written, ragged book, *The Pirate*, the figure of Cleveland—cast up by the sea on the resounding foreland of Dunrossness—moving, with the blood on his hands and the Spanish words on his tongue, among the simple islanders—singing a serenade under the window of his Shetland mistress—is conceived in the very highest manner of romantic invention. The words of his song, "Through groves of palm," sung in such a scene and by such a lover, clench, as in a nutshell, the emphatic contrast upon which the tale is built. In *Guy Mannering*, again, every incident is delightful to the imagination; and the scene when Harry Bertram lands at Ellangowan is a model instance of romantic method.

"'I remember the tune well,' he says, 'though I cannot guess what should at present so strongly recall it to my memory.'—He took his flageolet from his pocket and played a simple melody. Apparently the tune awoke the corresponding associations of a damsel. . . . She immediately took up the song—

> "'Are these the links of Forth, she said;
> Or are they the crooks of Dee,
> Or the bonny woods of Warroch Head
> That I so fain would see?'

"'By heaven!' said Bertram, 'it is the very ballad.'"

On this quotation two remarks fall to be made. First, as an instance of modern feeling for romance, this famous touch of the flageolet and the old song is selected by Miss Braddon for omission. Miss Braddon's idea of a story, like Mrs. Todgers's idea of a wooden leg, were something strange to have expounded. As a matter of personal experience, Meg's appearance to old

Mr. Bertram on the road, the ruins of Derncleugh, the scene of the flageolet, and the Dominie's recognition of Harry, are the four strong notes that continue to ring in the mind after the book is laid aside. The second point is still more curious. The reader will observe a mark of excision in the passage as quoted by me. Well, here is how it runs in the original: "a damsel, who, close behind a fine spring about half-way down the descent, and which had once supplied the castle with water, was engaged in bleaching linen." A man who gave in such copy would be discharged from the staff of a daily paper. Scott has forgotten to prepare the reader for the presence of the "damsel"; he has forgotten to mention the spring and its relation to the ruin; and now, face to face with his omission, instead of trying back and starting fair, crams all this matter, tail foremost, into a single shambling sentence. It is not merely bad English, or bad style; it is abominably bad narrative besides.

Certainly the contrast is remarkable; and it is one that throws a strong light upon the subject of this paper. For here we have a man of the finest creative instinct touching with perfect certainty and charm the romantic junctures of his story; and we find him utterly careless, almost, it would seem, incapable, in the technical matter of style, and not only frequently weak, but frequently wrong in points of drama. In character parts, indeed, and particularly in the Scotch, he was delicate, strong and truthful;

but the trite, obliterated features of too many of his heroes have already wearied two generations of readers. At times his characters will speak with something far beyond propriety with a true heroic note; but on the next page they will be wading wearily forward with an ungrammatical and undramatic rigmarole of words. The man who could conceive and write the character of Elspeth of the Craigburnfoot, as Scott has conceived and written it, had not only splendid romantic, but splendid tragic gifts. How comes it, then, that he could so often fob us off with languid, inarticulate twaddle?

It seems to me that the explanation is to be found in the very quality of his surprising merits. As his books are play to the reader, so were they play to him. He conjured up the romantic with delight, but he had hardly patience to describe it. He was a great day-dreamer, a seer of fit and beautiful and humorous visions, but hardly a great artist; hardly, in the manful sense, an artist at all. He pleased himself, and so he pleases us. Of the pleasures of his art he tasted fully; but of its toils and vigils and distresses never man knew less. A great romantic—an idle child.

XVI

A Humble Remonstrance *

I

WE have recently † enjoyed a quite peculiar pleasure: hearing, in some detail, the opinions, about the art they practise, of Mr. Walter Besant and Mr. Henry James; two men certainly of very different calibre: Mr. James so precise of outline, so cunning of fence, so scrupulous of finish, and Mr. Besant so genial, so friendly, with so persuasive and humorous a vein of whim: Mr. James the very type of the deliberate artist, Mr. Besant the impersonation of good nature. That such doctors should differ will excite no great surprise; but one point in which they seem to agree fills me, I confess, with wonder. For they are both content to talk about the "art of fiction"; and Mr. Besant, waxing exceedingly bold, goes on to oppose this so-called "art of fiction" to the "art of poetry." By the art of poetry he can mean nothing but the art of verse,

* This paper, which does not otherwise fit the present volume, is reprinted here as the proper continuation of the last.

† 1884.

an art of handicraft, and only comparable with the art of prose. For that heat and height of sane emotion which we agree to call by the name of poetry, is but a libertine and vagrant quality; present, at times, in any art, more often absent from them all; too seldom present in the prose novel, too frequently absent from the ode and epic. Fiction is in the same case; it is no substantive art, but an element which enters largely into all the arts but architecture. Homer, Wordsworth, Phidias, Hogarth, and Salvini, all deal in fiction; and yet I do not suppose that either Hogarth or Salvini, to mention but these two, entered in any degree into the scope of Mr. Besant's interesting lecture or Mr. James's charming essay. The art of fiction, then, regarded as a definition, is both too ample and too scanty. Let me suggest another; let me suggest that what both Mr. James and Mr. Besant had in view was neither more nor less than the art of narrative.

But Mr. Besant is anxious to speak solely of "the modern English novel," the stay and bread-winner of Mr. Mudie; and in the author of the most pleasing novel on that roll, *All Sorts and Conditions of Men*, the desire is natural enough. I can conceive, then, that he would hasten to propose two additions, and read thus: the art of *fictitious* narrative *in prose*.

Now the fact of the existence of the modern English novel is not to be denied; materially, with its three volumes, leaded type, and gilded lettering, it is easily distinguishable from other forms of literature; but to talk at all fruitfully of any branch of art, it is needful to build our definitions on some more fundamental ground than binding. Why, then, are we to add "in prose"? *The Odyssey* appears to me the best of romances; *The Lady of the Lake* to stand high in the second order; and Chaucer's tales and prologues to contain more of the matter and art of the modern English novel than the whole treasury of Mr. Mudie. Whether a narrative be written in blank verse or the Spenserian stanza, in the long period of Gibbon or the chipped phrase of Charles Reade, the principles of the art of narrative must be equally observed. The choice of a noble and swelling style in prose affects the problem of narration in the same way, if not to the same degree, as the choice of measured verse; for both imply a closer synthesis of events, a higher key of dialogue, and a more picked and stately strain of words. If you are to refuse *Don Juan*, it is hard to see why you should include *Zanoni* or (to bracket works of very different value) *The Scarlet Letter;* and by what discrimination are you to open your doors to *The Pilgrim's Progress* and close them on *The Faery Queen?* To bring things closer home, I will here propound to Mr. Besant a conundrum. A narrative called *Paradise Lost* was written in English verse by one John Milton; what was it then? It was next translated by Chateaubriand into French prose; and what was it then? Lastly, the French translation was, by some inspired compatriot of George Gilfillan (and of mine) turned bodily into an English novel; and, in the name of clearness, what was it then?

But, once more, why should we add "fictitious"? The reason why is obvious. The reason why not, if something more recondite, does not want for weight. The art of narrative, in fact, is the same, whether it is applied to the selection and illustration of a real series of events or of an imaginary series. Boswell's *Life of Johnson* (a work of cunning and inimitable art) owes its success to the same technical manœuvres as (let us say) *Tom Jones*: the clear conception of certain characters of man, the choice and presentation of certain incidents out of a great number that offered, and the invention (yes, invention) and preservation of a certain key in dialogue. In which these things are done with the more art—in which with the greater air of nature—readers will differently judge. Boswell's is, indeed, a very special case, and almost a generic; but it is not only in Boswell, it is in every biography with any salt of life, it is in every history where events and men, rather than ideas, are presented—in Tacitus, in Carlyle, in Michelet, in Macaulay—that the novelist will find many of his own methods most conspicuously and adroitly handled. He will find besides that he, who is free—who has the right to invent or steal a missing incident, who has the right, more precious still, of wholesale omission—is frequently defeated, and, with all his advantages, leaves a less strong impression of reality and passion. Mr. James utters his mind with a becoming fervour on the sanctity of truth to the novelist; on a more careful examination truth will seem a word of very debatable propriety, not only for the labours of the novelist, but for those of the historian. No art—to use the daring phrase of Mr. James—can successfully "compete with life"; and the art that seeks to do so is condemned to perish *montibus aviis.* Life goes before us, infinite in complication; attended by the most various and surprising meteors; appealing at once to the eye, to the ear, to the mind—the seat of wonder, to the touch—so thrillingly delicate, and to the belly—so imperious when starved. It combines and employs in its manifestation the method and material, not of one art only, but of all the arts. Music is but an arbitrary trifling with a few of life's majestic chords; painting is but a shadow of its pageantry of light and colour; literature does but drily indicate that wealth of incident, of moral obligation, of virtue, vice, action, rapture and agony, with which it teems. To "compete with life," whose sun we cannot look upon, whose passions and diseases waste and slay us—to compete with the flavour of wine, the beauty of the dawn, the scorching of fire, the bitterness of death and separation—here is, indeed, a projected escalade of heaven; here are, indeed, labours for a Hercules in a dress coat, armed with a pen and a dictionary to depict the passions, armed with a tube of superior flake-white to paint the portrait of the insufferable sun. No art is true in this sense: none can "compete with life"; not even history, built indeed of indisputable facts, but these facts robbed of their vivacity and sting; so that even when we read of the sack of a city or the fall of an empire, we are surprised, and justly commend the author's talent, if our pulse be quickened. And mark, for a last differentia, that this quickening of the pulse is, in almost every case, purely agreeable; that these phantom reproductions of experience, even at their most acute, convey decided pleasure; while experience itself, in the cockpit of life, can torture and slay.

What, then, is the object, what the method, of an art, and what the source of its power? The whole secret is that no art does "compete with life." Man's one method, whether he reasons or creates, is to half-shut his eyes against the dazzle and confusion of reality. The arts, like arithmetic and geometry, turn away their eyes from the gross, coloured and mobile nature at our feet, and regard instead a certain figmentary abstraction. Geometry will tell us of a circle, a thing never seen in nature; asked about a green circle or an iron circle, it lays its hand upon its mouth. So with the arts. Painting, ruefully comparing sunshine and flake-white, gives up truth of colour, as it had already given up relief and movement; and instead of vying with nature, arranges a scheme of harmonious tints. Literature, above all in its most typical mood, the mood of narrative, similarly flees the direct challenge and pursues instead an independent and creative aim. So far as it imitates at all, it imitates not life but speech: not the facts of human destiny, but the emphasis and the suppressions with which the human actor tells of them. The real art that dealt with life directly was that of the first men who told their stories round the savage camp-fire. Our art is occupied, and bound to be occupied, not so much in making stories true as in making them typical; not so much in capturing the lineaments of each fact, as in marshalling all of them towards a common end. For the welter of impressions, all forcible but all discreet, which life presents, it substitutes a certain artificial series of impressions, all indeed most feebly represented, but all aiming at the same effect, all eloquent of the same idea, all chiming together like consonant notes in music or like the graduated tints in a good picture. From all its chapters, from all its pages, from all its sentences, the well-written novel echoes and re-echoes its one creative and controlling thought; to this must every incident and character contribute; the style must have been pitched in unison with this; and if there is anywhere a word that looks another way, the book would be stronger, clearer, and (I had almost said) fuller without it. Life is monstrous, infinite, illogical, abrupt and poignant; a work of art, in comparison, is neat, finite, self-contained, rational, flowing and emasculate. Life imposes by brute energy, like inarticulate thunder; art catches the ear, among the far louder noises of experience, like an air artificially made by a discreet musician. A proposition of geometry does not compete with life ; and a proposition of geometry is a fair and luminous parallel for a work of art. Both are reasonable, both untrue to the crude fact ; both inhere in nature, neither represents it. The novel, which is a work of art, exists, not by its resemblances to life, which are forced and material, as a shoe must still consist of leather, but by its immeasurable difference from life, which is designed and significant, and is both the method and the meaning of the work.

The life of man is not the subject of novels, but the inexhaustible magazine from which subjects are to be selected; the name of these is legion; and with each new subject—for here again I must differ by the whole width of heaven from Mr. James—the true artist will vary his method and change the point of attack. That which was in one case an excellence, will become a defect in another ; what was the making of one book, will in the next be impertinent or dull. First each novel, and then each class of novels, exists by and for itself. I will take, for instance, three main classes, which are fairly distinct: first, the novel of adventure, which appeals to certain almost sensual and quite illogical tendencies in man ; second, the novel of character, which appeals to our intellectual appreciation of man's foibles and mingled and inconstant motives ; and third, the dramatic novel, which deals with the same stuff as the serious theatre, and appeals to our emotional nature and moral judgment.

And first for the novel of adventure. Mr. James refers, with singular generosity of praise, to a little book about a quest for hidden treasure; but he lets fall, by the way, some rather startling words. In this book he misses what he calls the "immense luxury" of being able to quarrel with his author. The luxury, to most of us, is to lay by our judgment, to be submerged by the tale as by a billow, and only to awake, and begin to distinguish and find fault, when the piece is over and the volume laid aside. Still more remarkable is Mr. James's reason. He cannot criticise the author, as he goes, "because," says he, comparing it with another work, "*I have been a child, but I have never been on a quest for buried treasure.*" Here is, indeed, a wilful paradox; for if he has never been on a quest for buried treasure, it can be demonstrated that he has never been a child. There never was a child (unless Master James) but has hunted gold, and been a pirate, and a military commander, and a bandit of the mountains; but has fought, and suffered shipwreck and prison, and imbrued its little hands in gore, and gallantly retrieved the lost battle, and triumphantly protected innocence and beauty. Elsewhere in his essay Mr. James has protested with excellent reason against too narrow a conception of experience; for the born artist, he contends, the "faintest hints of life" are converted into revelations; and it will be found true, I believe, in a majority of cases, that the artist writes with more gusto and effect of those things which he has only wished to do, than of those which he has done. Desire is a wonderful telescope, and Pisgah the best observatory. Now, while it is true that neither Mr. James nor the author of the work in question has ever, in the fleshly sense, gone questing after gold, it is probable that both have ardently desired and fondly imagined the details of such a life in youthful day-dreams; and the author, counting upon that, and well aware (cunning and low-minded man!) that this class of interest, having been frequently treated, finds a readily accessible and beaten road to the sympathies of the reader, addressed himself throughout to the building up and circumstantiation of this boyish dream. Character to the boy is a sealed book; for him, a pirate is a beard, a pair of wide trousers and a liberal complement of pistols. The author, for the sake of circumstantiation and because he was himself more or less grown up, admitted character, within certain limits, into his design; but only within certain limits. Had the same puppets figured in a scheme of another sort, they had been drawn to very different purpose; for in this elementary novel of adventure, the characters need to be presented with but one class of qualities—the warlike and formidable. So as they appear insidious in deceit and fatal in the combat, they have served their end. Danger is the matter with which this class of novel deals; fear, the passion with which it idly trifles; and the characters are portrayed only so far as they realise the sense of danger and provoke the sympathy of fear. To add more traits, to be too clever, to start the hare of moral or intellectual interest while we are running the fox of material interest, is not to enrich but to stultify your tale. The stupid reader will only be offended, and the clever reader lose the scent.

The novel of character has this difference from all others: that it requires no coherency of plot, and for this reason, as in the case of *Gil Blas*, it is sometimes called the novel of adventure. It turns on the humours of the persons represented; these are, to be sure, embodied in incidents, but the incidents themselves, being tributary, need not march in a progression; and the characters may be statically shown. As they enter, so they may go out; they must be consistent, but they need not grow. Here Mr. James will recognise the note of much of his own work: he treats, for the most part, the statics of character, studying it at rest or only gently moved; and, with his usual delicate and just artistic instinct, he avoids those stronger passions which would deform the attitudes he loves to study, and change his sitters from the humorists of ordinary life to the brute forces and bare types of more emotional moments. In his recent *Author of Beltraffio*, so just in conception, so nimble and neat in workmanship, strong passion is indeed employed ; but observe that it is not displayed. Even in the heroine the working of the passion is suppressed ; and the great struggle, the true tragedy, the *scène-à-faire*, passes unseen behind the panels of a locked door. The delectable invention of the young visitor is introduced, consciously or not, to this end : that Mr. James, true to his method, might avoid the scene of passion. I trust no reader will suppose me guilty of undervaluing this little masterpiece. I mean merely that it belongs to one marked class of novel, and that it would have been very differently conceived and treated had it belonged to that other marked class, of which I now proceed to speak.

I take pleasure in calling the dramatic novel by that name, because it enables me to point out by the way a strange and peculiarly English misconception. It is sometimes supposed that the drama consists of incident. It consists of passion, which gives the actor his opportunity ; and that passion must progressively increase, or the actor as the piece proceeded, would be unable to carry the audience from a lower to a higher pitch of interest and emotion. A good serious play must therefore be founded on one of the passionate *cruces* of life, where duty and inclination come nobly to the grapple ; and the same is true of what I call, for that reason, the dramatic novel. I will instance a-few worthy specimens, all of our own day and language ; Meredith's *Rhoda Fleming*, that wonderful and painful book, long out of print,* and hunted for at bookstalls like an Aldine; Hardy's *Pair of Blue Eyes;* and two of Charles Reade's, *Griffith Gaunt* and *The Double Marriage*, originally called *White Lies*, and founded (by an accident quaintly favourable to my nomenclature) on a play by Maquet, the partner of the great Dumas. In this kind of novel the closed door of *The Author of Beltraffio* must be broken open; passion must appear upon the scene and utter its last word; passion is the be-all and the end-all, the plot and the solution, the protagonist and the *deus ex machinâ* in one. The characters may come anyhow upon the stage: we do not care; the point is, that, before they leave it, they shall become transfigured and raised out of themselves by passion. It may be part of the design to draw them with detail; to depict a full-length character, and then behold it melt and change in the furnace of emotion. But there is no obligation of the sort; nice portraiture is not required; and we are content to accept mere abstract types, so they be strongly and sincerely moved. A novel of this class may be even great, and yet contain no individual figure; it may be great, because it displays the workings of the perturbed heart and the impersonal utterance of passion; and with an artist of the second class it is, indeed, even more likely to be great, when the issue has thus been narrowed and the whole force of the writer's mind directed to passion alone. Cleverness again,

* Now no longer so, thank Heaven!

which has its fair field in the novel of character, is debarred all entry upon this more solemn theatre. A far-fetched motive, an ingenious evasion of the issue, a witty instead of a passionate turn, offend us like an insincerity. All should be plain, all straightforward to the end. Hence it is that, in *Rhoda Fleming*, Mrs. Lovell raises such resentment in the reader; her motives are too flimsy, her ways are too equivocal, for the weight and strength of her surroundings. Hence the hot indignation of the reader when Balzac, after having begun the *Duchesse de Langeais* in terms of strong if somewhat swollen passion, cuts the knot by the derangement of the hero's clock. Such personages and incidents belong to the novel of character; they are out of place in the high society of the passions; when the passions are introduced in art at their full height, we look to see them, not baffled and impotently striving, as in life, but towering above circumstance and acting substitutes for fate.

And here I can imagine Mr. James, with his lucid sense, to intervene. To much of what I have said he would apparently demur; in much he would, somewhat impatiently, acquiesce. It may be true; but it is not what he desired to say or to hear said. He spoke of the finished picture and its worth when done; I, of the brushes, the palette, and the north light. He uttered his views in the tone and for the ear of good society; I, with the emphasis and technicalities of the obtrusive student. But the point, I may reply, is not merely to amuse the public, but to offer helpful advice to the young writer. And the young writer will not so much be helped by genial pictures of what an art may aspire to at its highest, as by a true idea of what it must be on the lowest terms. The best that we can say to him is this : Let him choose a motive, whether of character or passion ; carefully construct his plot so that every incident is an illustration of the motive, and every property employed shall bear to it a near relation of congruity or contrast ; avoid a sub-plot, unless, as sometimes in Shakespeare, the sub-plot be a reversion or complement of the main intrigue ; suffer not his style to flag below the level of the argument ; pitch the key of conversation, not with any thought of how men talk in parlours, but with a single eye to the degree of passion he may be called on to express ; and allow neither himself in the narrative nor any character in the course of the dialogue, to utter one sentence that is not part and parcel of the business of the story or the discussion of the problem involved. Let him not regret if this shortens his book ; it will be better so ; for to add irrelevant matter is not to lengthen but to bury. Let him not mind if he miss a thousand qualities, so that he keeps unflaggingly in pursuit of the one he has chosen. Let him not care particularly if he miss the tone of conversation, the pungent material detail of the day's manners, the reproduction of the atmosphere and the environment. These elements are not essential ;

a novel may be excellent, and yet have none of them; a passion or a character is so much the better depicted as it rises clearer from material circumstance. In this age of the particular, let him remember the ages of the abstract, the great books of the past, the brave men that lived before Shakespeare and before Balzac. And as the root of the whole matter, let him bear in mind that his novel is not a transcript of life, to be judged by its exactitude; but a simplification of some side or point of life, to stand or fall by its significant simplicity. For although, in great men, working upon great motives what we observe and admire is often their complexity, yet underneath appearances the truth remains unchanged: that simplification was their method, and that simplicity is their excellence.

II

Since the above was written another novelist has entered repeatedly the lists of theory: one well worthy of mention, Mr. W. D. Howells; and none ever couched a lance with narrower convictions. His own work and those of his pupils and masters singly occupy his mind; he is the bond-slave, the zealot of his school; he dreams of an advance in art like what there is in science; he thinks of past things as radically dead; he thinks a form can be outlived: a strange immersion in his own history; a strange forgetfulness of the history of the race! Meanwhile, by a glance at his own works (could he see them with the eager eyes of his readers) much of this illusion would be dispelled. For while he holds all the poor little orthodoxies of the day—no poorer and no smaller than those of yesterday or to-morrow, poor and small, indeed, only so far as they are exclusive—the living quality of much that he has done is of a contrary, I had almost said of a heretical, complexion. A man, as I read him, of an originally strong romantic bent—a certain glow of romance still resides in many of his books, and lends them their distinction. As by accident he runs out and revels in the exceptional; and it is then, as often as not, that his reader rejoices—justly, as I contend. For in all this excessive eagerness to be centrally human, is there not one central human thing that Mr. Howells is too often tempted to neglect: I mean himself? A poet, a finished artist, a man in love with the appearances of life, a cunning reader of the mind, he has other passions and aspirations than those he loves to draw. And why should he suppress himself and do such reverence to the Lemuel Barkers? The obvious is not of necessity the normal; fashion rules and deforms; the majority fall tamely into the contemporary shape, and thus attain, in the eyes of the true observer, only a higher power of insignificance; and the danger is lest, in seeking to draw the normal, a man should draw the null, and write the novel of society instead of the romance of man.